I watch eight Canadian geese in a low tight vee hunkered against the western sky steadily winging their way northward. Beams of the rising sun bounce off their dark wings and white bellies. ...Without looking back, I pick up the buckets of slop and trudge to the hog pens wondering what those geese will see before the day ends and where they will sleep tonight.

* * * * *

Ma was tougher than my dad thought. He always said she needed protecting. From what? I wondered. She could touch a hot iron and not cry.

* * * * *

I was married at the age of seven. The wedding took place on a Friday night in the shadows of Ben's store.

* * * * *

Tip, my four-footed hunting companion, sniffs the air just above the bent grass. We move forward into a cavernous gravel pit. Here dragons could still roam. With pebbles in hand on tiptoes, I and my dog move ever so slowly so as not to scare off any animal lurking about.

* * * * *

We had central heating in the original farmhouse. That meant there was a large iron grate in the floor between the living room and dining room that provided heat for the entire house.

Cow Pies & Bases

Cow Pies
&
Bases

Robert B. Coates

Singing River Publications
Ely, Minnesota

Copyright © 2003 by Robert B. Coates

Edited by:
  Betty Vos and Charles Morello

Produced by:
  Charles Morello
  IRIS Enterprises
  Eveleth, MN 55734

Published by:
  Singing River Publications
  P.O. Box 72
  Ely, MN 55731
  www.speravi.com/singingriver

Printed by:
  Arrowhead Printing Inc
  625 Hughitt Avenue
  Superior, WI 54880

"Old Woman Fishing" first published in *Grit: American Life and Traditions*, April 2, 2000. Reprinted by permission.

This book is published in the United States of America by Singing River Publications, Ely, Minnesota. No portion of this book may be reproduced, stored in or introduced into a retrieval system, or transmitted, in any form or by any means — including photocopying — without the prior written permission of Robert B. Coates, except in the case of brief quotations embodied in critical articles and reviews. For information, address inquiries to Singing River Publications, P.O. Box 72, Ely, MN, 55731

ISBN: 0-9709575-8-0

1. Wisconsin History; 2. Country Humor; 3. Midwest Region; 4. Rural Culture; 5. Dairy Farming; 6. Childhood Reminiscences; 7. Americana

TO MY PARENTS

ARCHIE & BERNICE COATES

AND TO MY TEACHER

ANNA DIRKSE

ACKNOWLEDGEMENTS

Although I had written hundreds of sermons and nearly a hundred academic publications, I suffered a kind of writer's block when it came to writing fiction and creative non-fiction.

Until, that is, I stumbled into a writing workshop led by Pat Schneider in 1994. It is her belief that each of us is a writer with many stories to tell. With Pat's patient nudging, along with encouragement from other writers in the group, my personal stories began to spill onto the page. Fourteen of the pieces appearing in *Cow Pies & Bases* were first drafted in one of three such workshops or in her Creative Writing Workshop Leadership course. To Pat Schneider, founder and director of Amherst Writers and Artists and author of *The Writer as an Artist*, I owe a deep debt of gratitude.

I also wish to thank Chuck Morello, who has provided valuable editorial assistance in preparing *Cow Pies* for publication. His creativity has markedly improved this total effort.

Thanks to Chris Moroni, of Singing River Publications, for her valuable experience, and also for serving as a reminder that what we write really does matter.

To my wife and co-conspirator, Betty Vos, I must say thank you for your steadfast encouragement, your editorial skill, and your willingness to take risks so these stories might be read by others.

And to family and friends, thanks for being there along the way, shaping and sharing stories.

TABLE OF CONTENTS

ACKNOWLEDGEMENTS iii
INTRODUCTION vii

1. COW PIES & BASES 1
2. MY WORLD 3
3. BEN'S STORE 7
4. MAIL CALL 9
5. OUR FARM 11
6. THROUGH THE BARN DOOR................... 13
7. A WISE MAN 15
8. 222 17
9. THE END OF AN ERA 19
10. MY BIKE 23
11. OUR FARMHOUSE 25
12. THE TRACTOR 29
13. IRONING 31
14. THE KITCHEN TABLE 33
15. A HERD OF MY OWN 35
16. GRANDPA 37
17. WORK HORSES 39
18. GRADE SCHOOL TEACHER 43
19. SUNDAY AFTERNOONS 45
20. HUNTER RABBIT 47
21. MEASLES, CHICKEN POX, AND MUMPS 49
22. GRANDMA 51
23. FERRIS WHEEL 53
24. BELL RINGING 55
25. TV COMES TO OUR HOUSE 57
26. COW TANK 61
27. CHESTNUT TREES 63

28. COUNTY FAIR	65
29. THE LIBRARY	69
30. CHOPPING ICE	71
31. WINTER DREAMS	73
32. SCHOOLYARD BULLIES	75
33. GROWING THE HERD	77
34. WEIGHING MUSICAL SCALES	81
35. IN THE STARS	85
36. GEESE FLY NORTH	87
37. BIRTH AT TWENTY BELOW	89
38. SHOW AND TELL	93
39. SCHOOLHOUSE DISCIPLINE	95
40. BOYS AND GIRLS	99
41. OLD WOMAN FISHING	101
42. WORRY	103
43. RAKING HAY	105
44. PUBLIC SPEAKING	107
45. SHEPHERDS QUAKE	109
46. CRAYONS ON A DESK	113
47. NEAR MISSES	115
48. PREACHING TO THE COWS	119
49. THE SILO	123
50. LEFTOVERS!	125
51. CHRISTMAS EVE	127
52. THE FUNERAL	131
53. CHURCH SOCIALS	133
54. SNAKES ALIVE	135
55. PUSSY WILLOW	137
56. THE BARN REVISITED	139

INTRODUCTION

The primary cauldron for my growing up years was the farm. There was also the farm community with its one room schoolhouse, community church and four corners grocery store. Growing up on a farm involved each of those as well as the people who taught and learned, who prayed for good weather and good health, who bought their groceries while swapping stories and local gossip. From 4-H to MYF, from school plays to pastureland baseball fields, from stories of my grandparents to sharing pre-adolescent dreams while perched on the broad limb of an oak tree — through a mixing and sorting of all of these, like the ancient winnowing ways of sifting wheat from chaff, rural values and rural culture were breathed into my body merging with tissue and bone, shaping and becoming an ever present element of my heart. It was the farm, however, where all the puzzle pieces of coming of age had to fit together.

Cow Pies & Bases is a collection of vignettes or short stories emerging from my childhood. They cover the decade from when I was three or four years old until I graduated from eighth grade. When I first began to write them, they were just personal stories that made family members laugh and cry. Then I started to share them with local church groups and literary groups, and those audiences laughed and cried, too. It was at that point that I realized my youngest son was right when he said, "Dad, you need to get those stories out there — it's much bigger than just you and your childhood."

Others have told me that the stories are windows onto a life that doesn't exist anymore and therefore should be preserved. I agree that we have moved far, far beyond the late 1940s and 1950s technologically, but I expect that many of the same existential quandaries that children grappled with growing up in a farm community during that period continue to challenge their counterparts generations later in radically different settings. Fear, hubris, quest for meaning, sexual curiosity, who am I, why me, why this family, what's beyond me, will I measure up, and what does the future hold are feelings and questions that gnaw at the lives of all kids, both yesterday and today.

Thus this work is more than nostalgia. It does not attempt to glamorize rural life, but rather attempts to describe it with many of its rougher edges exposed for others to make what they will of them. These stories provide a peek at what it was like to grow up at a time when farm technology was still in a stage of infancy. Farm work during the years described here moved from depending on horses to relying solely on machines. Women who had worked much of the time beside their husbands in the fields and barns gradually took their places in the house, leaving the animals and land to the men. Children who could point to past generations that had remained on the farm now began to leave in droves — the land was no longer the place of opportunity.

Yet, can one really leave the land?

If the stories in this collection are to be believed, I expect the answer is a resounding "no." Those of us who grew up in the country remain part of that experience, just as those who grew up in towns and cities remain part of that experience. We can physically leave, we can emotionally leave, but there remains a deep spiritual link to the places that birthed us.

But, lest we get too serious, I must remind myself and those who read these stories that they were initially written to tell a story and to entertain. That means there will be ample moments for laughter and for tears, because entertainment is composed of both comedy and tragedy.

And, I hope that these stories will, from time to time, cause moments of reflection, not only about the past, but also about the future.

***

While the setting for these stories is real, the names of individuals are fictitious. Occasionally, changes in the setting are even made to further disguise characters. Are the stories true? They are as I remember them. There may be no other person in the community or even in my family who will remember them in the same way, but they are lodged in my memory as such, and so are as true as most stories handed down from one generation to the next. The intent here is not to write history, but to share the flavor of growing up in a Midwest farm community during the late 1940s and '50s.

x

1: COW PIES AND BASES

In my youth, we played baseball in a pasture. Bases were usually well-dried cow pies. Well-dried was more important than size. One afternoon, Jimmy Boscoe showed up with real bases. His dad had put sand in four flour bags. They looked better than cow pies, but were dangerous when we slid in fast and hard.

In the fourth, Jimmy hit a long drive toward me in right field. Being the greedy guy he was, he tried to stretch a sure double into an uncertain triple. My arm was stronger than his legs, if not his brain. He was out by at least two big feet. Jimmy complained. He cussed. He bawled. "They're my bases," he hollered. "I was safe!"

"The hell you say. You're out!" Both teams agreed with the ump. Boscoe grabbed the bases and ran home. The search was on for four cow pies. Well-dried was more important than size.

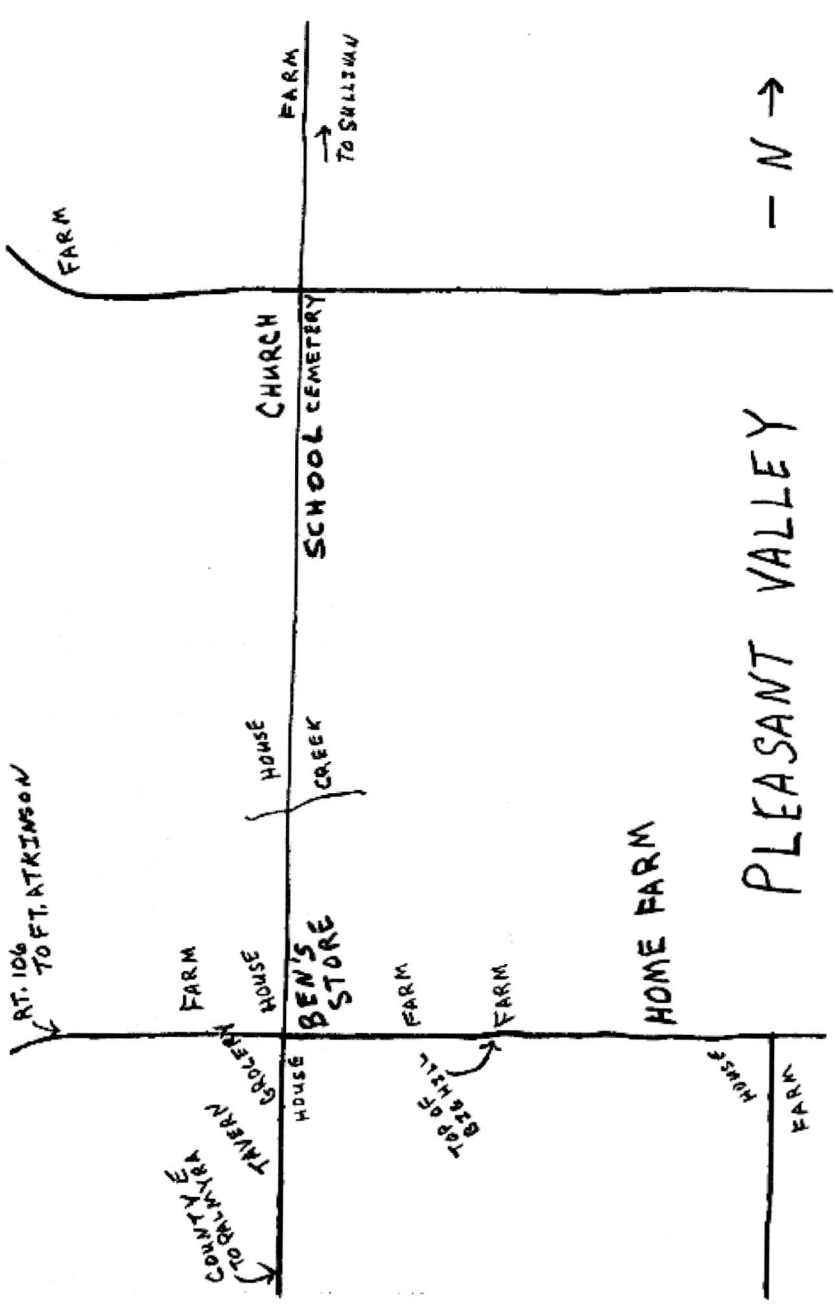

2: MY WORLD

Until I went to high school four miles away from home, my world was defined largely by one mile of blacktop. We lived on Highway 106. Turning right at the end of our driveway — seldom did I ever turn left — I could walk or ride my bike a half mile downhill past two farms on the right (there were no buildings on the left) until I reached the four corners where 106 crossed County E.

There, on my right, was Ben's grocery store and home; he also sold some farm implements. On my left was a house; in its yard the owners kept a few goats. Across from the house was a bar with an attached living area. Next to it, on 106, was a building that during my grade school years was turned into a grocery store. And across from it were a house and a defunct creamery.

Oak Hill was the official name of the four corners, but few locals called it that. Its longer name was Pumpkin Hollow. I was told that in the old days a woman made the area famous for the pumpkin pies that she baked and cooled on her kitchen window sill. But Pumpkin Hollow was more words than most folks wanted to use, so the four corners was simply known as Punk.

At that four corner intersection, I'd turn right onto County E and walk or pedal another half mile past a couple houses and a couple more farms until I approached another four corners. At that intersection, open land comprised the two corners furthest from me. On my near left was the Pleasant Valley Methodist Church and on my right the Pleasant Valley Cemetery. Next to the cemetery, back toward Punk, stood one of the hubs of my young life: Pleasant Valley School.

Until I finished eighth grade, my world centered on that

road from the farm to the school and church and back to the farm. There were a few additional spokes. Another mile or so down County E from Punk were neighbors with whom we shared some of our farm work and who were very much part of our social lives. By turning left at the church, we would shortly come to a farm that raised sheep and purebred Holsteins. That was where I bought my first purebred calf. In those early years of my life, I did not know where the road led to if we had turned right or east at the church. I did know that if we continued on County E from Punk past the church for four miles we would arrive in Sullivan, where we did some banking and where another implement dealer was located.

Again, using the four corners at Punk as our compass, I had a friend who lived another half mile west on 106 and we would occasionally get together and play. If we turned left or south onto County E, we would arrive in Palmyra four miles down the road. At Palmyra were the feed mills, a dill pickle factory, the train depot and more farm implement dealers. There, we shopped for groceries that were not available at Ben's store. General clothing needs were taken care of there or in Fort Atkinson, fourteen miles further west on 106. Depending on seasonal demands on the farm, we might get to Palmyra every two to three weeks. Trips to Fort were much less frequent.

Our farm was located about thirty miles southwest of Milwaukee and thirty miles southeast of Madison. Those two cities might as well have been located on either coast; we were simply not oriented toward the "big cities." I remember going to a Milwaukee Braves game once and to the Wisconsin State Fair, held just outside of Milwaukee, a few times. I don't recall going to Madison with my family, though when I was in the third grade my grade school went there along with other area rural schools to see the state capitol, to tour a potato chip factory, and to see the Madison airport. It was there where I saw my first fighter jet and that was a thrill. When I was in grade school, if we heard the sound of a plane, we all stopped what we were doing to see if we could spot it.

Most years our school did an annual field trip. One of the more memorable occurred when I was in the fifth grade. We, again with students from other area rural schools, traveled to Chicago to tour the Museum of Science and Industry. In order to fill a bus several rural schools had to coordinate their field trips. The bus ride itself was novel because most of us had never been on a bus before. And most of us had never been to a museum. It was huge and noisy. The coal mine was dark and clammy. Decades later, I passed that museum daily going to and from work at the University of Chicago.

Another grade school trip for seventh and eighth graders only (our teacher could fit both classes into her car) took us to Prairie du Chien. This was the only overnight trip during those grade school years, and it was my first night away from family. This trip also involved ordering meals from menus at restaurants.

Our family made fairly regular three-day trips to north central Iowa where my grandmothers lived. We would get up at two in the morning and sometimes arrive at our destination just as folks there were drinking their first cup of morning coffee. My dad liked to drive in the early morning hours. It was probably easier with kids, and it meant less time away from the farm. I always enjoyed the smells of these early morning trips because I would usually start out in a brand new pair of Levi's. They smelled new, and of course there was the sharp aroma of my parents' coffee. On those trips, if we had started a bit later, we'd pull off into a schoolyard to eat the sandwiches my mother had brought along. On real special occasions, we'd stop at a restaurant in McGregor where I'd get a hamburger for breakfast. Now that was traveling first class!

It was difficult for dairy farmers to leave their herds for long, because cows can be quite finicky about who milks them. One Saturday, we left after morning milking to visit friends in Rockford, Illinois, and returned to the farm late Sunday night. When we opened the car doors, we were greeted by sounds of cows bellowing frantically in the cowyard. Cows are very particular about their milking schedule. If they are not milked within an hour or so of the same time each day, their udders enlarge with milk creating intense pressure which can lead to the hardening of the cow's udder, requiring medical intervention. The young man dad had hired to milk the herd had misunderstood when we would return and had not shown up to do the evening milking.

We had three extended family vacations during these grade school years. In 1951, we traveled with my grandmother to western Kansas, where my father was born and had spent his early years. We also went on to Colorado Springs and Pike's Peak. One of my grandmother's brothers worked on constructing the cog railroad up Pike's Peak. We have grainy black and white pictures of him and his crew dwarfed by huge snowdrifts. The two other family vacations were week-long fishing trips in northern Wisconsin.

These occasional trips were forays away from Punk and Pleasant Valley, expanding my world. When I went to high school, I discovered that I had actually traveled much more than many of my friends.

Still, it was that one mile stretch of road from the farm down the hill to Ben's store and then turning right to the school and church that most defined and shaped my childhood world.

3: BEN'S STORE

The pungent aromas of Ben's old country store slap you in the face upon entering: pickle brine, Swiss cheese, sausage, cinnamon, nutmeg. This section of the two room general mercantile is lined with canned vegetables, fruits, and milk. Dried meats dangle on hooks hanging from the ceiling.

As you move from the grocery to the room with the black wood stove at its center, you are greeted with contrasting smells. Wood smoke mixed with that of tobacco, used by slouched men swapping tales around card tables, and the stale cigar stench of butts left from the previous night's poker game hang heavily about. Yet the scents of freshly stocked Levi's, woolens, and leather goods still penetrate your nostrils.

Present also is that fragrance of which fantasies are made — of that brand new catcher's mitt which costs way too much.

A whiff of the freshly cut pine railing guides you upstairs to the mysteries of the loft. That wide open room under the rafters contains bolts, screws, washers, nails, and many gadgets that have no name. Several wall calendars catch your attention, but you must peek quickly before anyone catches you staring at the scantily clad women. Odors of grease and oil mingle with the mustiness of the eaves.

Ben's old country store was torn down long ago; aromatic memories linger still.

4: MAIL CALL

With eager anticipation, my mother awaited the approach of the mailman's car. Each day and every day she glanced up often from her work — whether it was cleaning, mending, or cooking — to see if it was time for the mail to arrive.

I don't know quite what it was about the mail that held such an attraction for her. There was little junk mail in those days, mainly bills and correspondence. Of course, she loved to receive letters. Rural life was often isolating. Mail call represented the possibility for contact with the outside world on a daily basis.

We did much of our shopping though catalogs — Sears & Roebuck, Spiegel, and Aldens. And if an order had been made, Ma would expect the package to arrive the following week, even though it normally took three or four weeks to reach us. Nonetheless, whether a package was expected or not, it seemed that for Ma each mail call had the potential for being a little Christmas.

I picked up Ma's zeal for mail at an early age. Watching for the mailman was like watching for the first robin in the spring. We made a game of it, Ma and I. Who would be the first to spy the mailman? Who could run the fastest to get to the mailbox? I'm sure it was a blow when my legs grew to the point that I could get there quickest.

Even as a teenager with many chores to perform around the barn and sheds, I would keep an eye out for the mailman. Sometimes, even then, I'd try to outrun Ma, but she often beat me. Of course, coming from the house, she didn't have as far to run.

It wasn't easy finding ways to receive my own mail. I could write either one of my grandmothers and usually get a response, but that was about it. Until I discovered the United States Government Printing Office — now there was a find! They offered free publications on almost any subject a kid could think of. I had them send me pamphlets and brochures on soil conservation, tree planting, raising sheep, building barns and catalogs of everything else they could make available. And I read most of what they sent. For a kid growing up in the 50s, the USGPO may have been the precursor to the Internet.

Second only to that massive source of information were universities. By the time I completed the eighth grade I had catalogs from over forty colleges. I always seriously informed each college office that I was a seventh or eighth grader seeking information on college requirements so I could plan my high school courses appropriately. There was, no doubt, more than one raised eyebrow or chuckle over my hand written letter, but I don't remember any institution — public or private — not responding.

Between the United States Government Printing Office and universities, I had much to look forward to at mail call. There was a world out there I had barely glimpsed. We listened to the radio when I was small. In the early fifties, we bought a twelve inch black and white TV. But even with that addition to the living room, there remained much mystery about far away places and how others lived.

Mail call connected me with that mystery and fueled even more dreams about what could be. And my mother was the catalyst behind my fascination with mail.

But not all went well with the mail. One of my greatest disappointments in life had to do with trusting the mail. Like many boys and girls of my day, I dutifully saved my coins, enclosed a box top from a cereal box and sent off for a Roy Rogers ring. I waited, and waited, and waited. The mailman never delivered my ring.

I am still waiting!

5: OUR FARM

Our farm consisted of one hundred and sixty acres in the gently rolling hills of southeastern Wisconsin. That was dairy country. Our pastureland was dotted with black and white Holsteins. During much of this decade, the herd consisted of approximately eighty head including calves, yearlings, heifers, and some forty milking cows. Toward the end of this period the number of milk cows more than doubled. From time to time we also raised hogs, sheep and even the much dreaded chickens.

Always, though, it was the dairy herd around which the tilling of soil, sweat and toil, hopes and fears revolved. The hours of the day were divided according to morning and evening milking chores. Birthing could interrupt meals, sleep, or plans to be away even for a few hours. Death within the herd was grieved often as deeply as that of the passing of any other loved one.

If you approached the farm on Highway 106 from the west, that is from Oak Hill, you would turn into the first driveway. The second driveway led to a small one-story white house, originally constructed for a tenant, that we rented out. It was the first driveway, however, which led to our large white two-story clapboard house and then on past a machine shed and to the red barn which sat parallel with the road. A large cowyard stretched past the machine shed and back toward the house. Two 40-foot concrete silos stood against the barn and in the cow yard. A windmill stood sentry beside the machine shed on the edge of the cow yard.

At the end of the driveway, then, stood the barn on the right. At its near or west end was an attached milkhouse where milk cans were cooled and milking machines cleaned. Next to the milkhouse and adjoining the machine shed was a granary containing oats and feed for the cattle. Across from the west end of the barn was a farrowing shed/calf shed. North of it was another machine shed, and north of that was a shed for heifers, sheep, or hogs, depending on what animals we were raising at any given time. East of this area stood a corn crib.

Extending from the shed were two cow pastures. A cattle water tank straddled the fence separating the pastures. From there one could look back toward the barn and see the dirt ramp leading to the haymow on its second floor. It was on that ramp that wagons entered so hay and straw could be stored. The shortest end of the haymow was used for straw, but it also contained a water storage tank pumped by the windmill. From the time I was old enough to listen, I was warned against going into the strawmow for fear that I would slip into the water tank and drown.

North of the barn and outlying pasture was a gravel pit. From its hill, you could see all of our land. This hill provided great space for fantasies as well as for sledding during the winter months. The hill was also used for grazing cattle. Beyond the hill was a twenty acre field and beyond that the terrain dropped precipitously to a marsh, wet and soggy with quicksand holes.

The rest of the land west and east of the barn was divided into five more fields. We rotated crops from corn, to oats, to alfalfa. Some years, we were able to sell extra corn as a cash crop. Other years, we had to buy more hay in order to feed the cows through the winter.

An apt description of the farm would be incomplete without acknowledging the annual crop which we never had to plant — rocks. Every spring, frost heaves managed to push more rocks toward the ground's surface. They would appear after plowing and disking. Before planting, they had to be picked up and removed so they would not damage bailers, cornbines, or combines. The fences separating our fields were lined with stacks of rocks attesting to the forces of nature and to the back-breaking work of farmers.

6: THROUGH THE BARN DOOR

Standing in the doorway of the barn, I see the cows that need to be fed, that need to be milked. They are white and black in color, and sixty in number.

Those closest to the door turn their heads in the stanchions to see who enters their space. There is a sense of recognition — perhaps it is a mere acknowledgment that I am a source of food. I like to believe we are friends.

Standing in the doorway, I also see the cats that curl themselves on the soft, yellow straw. They, too, take note. To them I am wanted and feared: wanted, as I share with them the milk from the cows; feared, that I might crush them with a tractor or wagon tire.

Standing in the doorway, I see much whiteness. The walls and posts are whitewashed. The floor is limed with whiteness that I had spread earlier in the day. There is much whiteness, just as these cows give much whiteness.

Standing in the doorway, I try to see the child in far away Chicago who will drink the milk that these cows will give. I wonder, does that child know of cows who look to open doors, of cats who fear a tractor wheel, or of a young farm boy who tries to imagine life in the distant city?

7: A WISE MAN

Dad always wanted to be a farmer. His early years were spent in western Kansas where he ranched with his father. When he was eleven, his dad died and he and his mother and older brother moved to north central Iowa. Because of hard times, he only completed the eighth grade. Then he went to work beside his mother plucking chickens in the poultry house.

When he was old enough Dad started working for the Great Western Railroad on a track crew. Later, after he married and built a small house in Clarion, he was offered the position of brakeman which would have been a stepping stone to a secure career as a railroader. Dad turned that job down to follow his dream of being a farmer.

When Dad and Ma moved to Illinois, he worked by day on the Rock Island Railroad and began slowly to build a small herd of dairy cattle and purchase some machinery, tending the farm before and after work. Then he quit the railroad job and worked another farmer's land on shares for two years. Finally, when I was two years old, with some help from an uncle, Dad was able to buy his own farm in Wisconsin. He was thirty one.

While my dad had little formal education, he was a wise man. I grew up hearing short, pithy proverbs which so often characterize many of the rural regions of the country from New England, to the Midwest, to the South, to the West.

My brother frequently complained that I was lucky; my dad countered: "You make your own luck by working hard with what's available to you." I imagine that's how he looked at his own life.

Two of his proverbs that have stayed with me have to do

with respecting people of different religious faiths. "What you believe about God is important to you. But don't think you got the only answer when it comes to God," Dad would say. And another little proverb he picked up along the way he'd quote was: "He who tills the soil knows God by whatever language and by whatever name."

Here were seeds of religious tolerance and respect. The reflective farmer's views of the world, and of God for that matter, are shaped by the land. Around the world farmers have this in common. They know the rhythms of the season, the struggles with too little rain or too much rain, the pride of helping something grow, the undying hope for the next crop, the next calf, the next foal. Because life and death struggles face each who tills the soil, it may not be surprising that many see themselves working in partnership with the same God whether they worship in a church, a temple or a mosque.

For any child there is the danger of remembering a father as being bigger than life or of attempting to fit him into a neatly idealized image.

Now my dad was a wise man, in part, because of his words about respecting other people's faith; his words of religious tolerance have been important to me throughout my life.

Did he live by those words? Most of the time yes, but ... in the late 1950s, in rural America as I began dating girls, another "wise proverb" of my father's was: "Don't date Catholic girls. They'll only try to convert you."

Oh, well. A wise man, if you could be somewhat wise and selective in your hearing.

8: 222

"What number are you calling?"
"222, please."
Fortunately, I did not have to use the telephone often. I never liked talking to the operator and I heard my parents complain so often about neighbors on the party line listening in to their conversations that I dreaded the phone. But there were occasions when I was at a 4-H Club meeting or more rarely at a friend's house when I would have to pick up the black phone, turn the crank on the box and wait for the operator's scratchy voice.

At least the number was easy to remember. I learned early on that 222 was my home number. I used to call it "toot, toot, toot." If a crisis occurred at school, where there was no phone, I was to ride my bike as fast as I could to Ben's store and call home. That crisis never happened.

Our phone was primarily a business phone. It was used to call the vet, the artificial inseminator, the feed mill, implement dealers and repair shops. My dad used it most often.

Ma used it to call committee members about church suppers, but she only rarely called a neighbor to have a social conversation. "If you want to feed the gossip mill, then use the phone," was the dictum I was raised with. Ma did not want to feed the gossip mill. But there were moments when the party line phone was used for impromptu conference calls — long before conference calls became a routine part of the business world.

9: THE END OF AN ERA

When they tore the old schoolhouse down I didn't go watch.

"Progress," they called it. School consolidation. We were among the last of the one room schoolhouses in the county. Progress caught up with Pleasant Valley School in the early 60s.

It had been more than a heartbeat of my existence for my life. Even before I started school the small white building stood as a beacon guiding me along the path of the unknown. We would run across the road from the church to play in the schoolyard. It had a teeter-totter, swings that I could not climb into and a huge slide that I was afraid to scale. And there were books in that building. My brother brought some home, but I never got to touch them. I could hardly wait to go to a place where they would give me my own books. When my parents went to PTA meetings I was dragged along. More than one night I fell asleep on a table while the adults discussed school business.

And then it was my turn to actually go to school! Two big trees stood at its circular entrance. The gravel driveway separated the school from the swing set buried in concrete. A water pump stood some distance from the building; it was the chore of older children to pump water and fill the bubbler each morning. The bubbler sat at one end of the vestibule or entryway that stretched across the front of the building, where coats and hats were hung and boots were left. A doorway into the main room was at each end of the vestibule.

Stepping into the room, one could see rows of wide desks — the kind that rested on slats. An entire row of seats was attached to the slats. Each desk had inkwells and room for two children. Bookshelves and displays of art work lined much of the back of the room. A raised stage some six inches tall crossed the front of the room. A student had to step up on the stage to write on the large blackboard which extended the full length of the stage. To one side of the stage sat the teacher's desk; a piano stood on the other side. A table with eight chairs sometimes was on the stage and at other times it was in the center of the room.

In the back left corner sat a black stove. Next to it was a small door that led to a garage and wood/coal shed. Outside a basketball hoop hung on a tree on the north side of the building. East of the schoolhouse was a small oblong baseball diamond. A cornfield cut off much of leftfield. And at either end of the playground stood matching pit toilets — boys on the north side and girls on the south side.

As I moved through the grades, progress came to the school in the form of free-standing desks, one for each student. The hectograph was replaced with a mimeograph. And the stove was modernized. But the bubbler stayed the same, and the pit toilets never changed — with exception of Halloween, that is, when they were tipped over. But they were easily righted and school went on the next morning as if nothing had happened.

Each year we would get some new supplies and materials, but I looked forward to reading the books that the students ahead of me had been reading aloud. One of the advantages of a one-room learning environment was that if you listened closely, you got to go over the same subject at least a couple times. It always seemed like the classes ahead of me were reading more interesting things, and I could hardly wait to advance to the next class.

The campaign for consolidation had been going on for years. My parents fought it while I was in school as did many other parents in the community. But they were told that their children's education was suffering because they didn't have all the modern conveniences of town school. Our globe was out of date. Our teacher did not have a four year degree. And our method of learning, with eight grades in one room, was outmoded, almost a throw back to a previous century. Parents were informed that their children would suffer, would be far behind those children who had the opportunity to go to elementary and junior high school in town.

Oddly, when it was my turn to go to high school, over half the students making up the honor roll came from rural one-room schoolhouses, even though they comprised far less than half the total class.

Progress. The shouts of the teacher encouraging children of all grades to get a hit and make it to first base, the whispers of eager children with an answer to a question, the voices of boys and girls reciting a poem from memory no longer echo on that small plot of land.

Much of the schoolyard has been returned to a farmer's field. The old pump stands rusted against time. If you look closely, you can still see the outline of the school building in the turf where the grass changes color.

Pleasant Valley School is now part of the Pleasant Valley Cemetery. Someday, I will take my place there again, for a last time: I will be buried in a plot near the northwest corner of the old schoolhouse.

10: MY BIKE

    A hand-me-down bicycle. I never did get one of my own. It was way too big for me, as my brother was about seven years older and it fit him just right. My dad lowered the seat and placed two-by-four blocks on the pedals.
    I could at least touch the pedals. It was certainly uncomfortable standing up to get started; dangerous, too. In those early days of learning to ride there were many bumps, many false beginnings, many bruises of fender and body. Yet within a month I rode the bike as if I were glued to it. The wind against my face as I sped down the big hill sometimes whipped my breath away. The manual brakes squeaked as I reached the stop sign at the bottom of the hill. There I was joined by two older girls and we three continued on our way to the one-room school house.
    That bike carried me through mud puddles, over gravel roads, away from bullies and always home. It was some years before I could ride the bike back up the big hill. I usually had to hop off half way up the hill and push it the rest of the way while trying to keep it from falling on me. Each year, I'd be able to ride the bike a little higher up the hill. Finally, lungs nearly bursting, I conquered the hill.
    Oddly, when I revisited that same hill a few years ago, it had shrunk so much that a kid could now probably ride a tricycle up without pausing to catch breath.
    What happened to the bicycle? I don't know. I've always imagined it being handed down to some new kid eager to pedal it home — but more likely it lies rusting in a long abandoned scrap heap on the back-forty.

11: OUR FARMHOUSE

We had central heating in the original farmhouse. That meant there was a large iron grate in the floor between the living room and dining room that provided heat for the entire house. On the coldest days, the oven was lit and its door opened to provide a little more warmth.

A pit toilet sat out back. That's where you could find old editions of the Sears catalog, seed catalogs, and whatever else provided paper with some substance. I never have like spiders; I imagine that comes from eyeing them from my wooden perch. But even that was better than having to use the chamber pot after dark.

A man delivered ice blocks in the wee hours of the morning. I never saw him, though I saw plenty of evidence that he had been there. The coal deliveries I did see. I had to stay back so as not to get in the way, but I did manage to watch one or sometimes two men shovel the coal from their truck through the basement window.

The basement, before the house was modernized, was honed out of dirt. There was a large black stove down there. That was also where Ma stored the many jars of tomatoes, beans, peas, peaches, pears, pickles (dill, sweet and watermelon) and corn that she'd canned. Potatoes were also somewhere down there in the dark. In an adjoining area was a cistern.

I avoided the basement at all costs. From the few times that I had been down there, I knew the wooden stairs to be rickety. The only light came from a couple naked light bulbs and you couldn't trust that they'd always turn on. And there were rodents down there — of all sizes. There were times when Ma wouldn't go down the stairs without Dad. He set traps — small ones and large ones. I tried not to think much about the basement.

The upstairs was also off limits. In those early years, there was no heat up there other than what made its way through a vent. There were two rooms. One at the top of the stairs was small and would become my brother's room. Then I definitely was not allowed upstairs! My grandmother stayed in the larger room during the winter months until I was much older and Grandma couldn't handle the stairs well. Then she took my room off the dining room and I moved upstairs, to my brother's dismay.

In those early years, a brand new large green cook stove took up much of the space in the kitchen. A hand water pump brought water up from a storage tank. Depending upon how much rainfall we had received, washing days might mean carrying water from the well that was halfway between the barn and the house. I often watched my mother work the wringer washing machine and then take the clothes out to the clothesline where she hung them to dry. In cold weather, long johns came back in the house board-stiff and had to melt and be redried over the iron grate before being folded and placed in dresser drawers.

My mother worked as long and hard in the house as my dad did in the barn and on the land to maintain that house, prepare meals, keep us in clean clothes as well as at times help with haying, silo filling, or cleaning the milking utensils in the milkhouse.

My brother and I were assigned chores as soon as we could be taught to carry out responsible tasks. My earliest chore was to help my mother dust. We usually did that on Saturday morning. Of course my responsibility was to take care of objects low to the floor. There were plenty of them. I liked the smell of the furniture polish. I often didn't get things quite clean enough for my mother's eye, but this was my first chore of many that would follow.

Being the younger child by some six and half years, I was

the one who had to take over household duties when my mother was sick. My dad called me the "Chief Cook and Bottle Washer." The title I imagine was supposed to inspire and reward me. It seemed like there were more dishes to do than meals to cook. I wasn't too thrilled with this role as my brother often teased me about being the girl in the family. The story was that my mother had wanted me to be a girl so was keeping me inside to do "girl things."

I don't know whether or not that was true, but I would eventually take my place doing chores in the barn and on the farm. My mother lost her assistant, though advancing technologies by that time had lightened her load or at least changed it dramatically.

12: THE TRACTOR

I remember the first time I drove a tractor by myself. I was eight years old. My father and brother had been planting oats in the twenty-acre field behind the gravel pit. It was a fairly flat field enclosed by barbed wire fence. Rocks and trees also formed a natural boundary.

The tractor was an old SC Case. Its shape was that of a large tricycle. Its color was faded red. The brakes were controlled by foot pedals while the clutch and accelerator were hand operated.

I had wanted to drive the tractor for some time; I expect it was some kind of rite of passage on the farm. Previously, I had driven several times with my dad riding beside or behind me. But that was not "really" driving the tractor or working the fields.

My dad believed that rolling oats would be the safest experience for my first solo effort. Cultivating corn would be too risky as any unplanned swerve could wipe out bushels of the future corn crop.

No, rolling oats would be much safer. Pulled by the tractor, then, was a roller. It was about ten feet long and two feet wide and maybe two feet high with a row of iron wheels that pressed newly sown oats into the soft dirt to prevent the seeds from being blown or washed immediately away. The work was a significant part of the process of sowing oats.

Mounting the tractor with a feel of exhilaration and pride, I received my final instructions. I was simply to drive the tractor and roller across the field, turn around and return to where my dad was standing.

With foot ready on the brake and increasing the throttle a bit, I let out the clutch and lurched forward. All was fine.

The tractor moved forward and the roller followed obediently behind.

Feeling quite good about my triumph, I neared the far fence. Beginning my turn, I moved to let the clutch out — instead, I pulled the gas throttle to its maximum speed.

Panic set in. I hit the brakes with little effect. I couldn't seem to find the clutch lever. I kept pulling the throttle lever instead. As a tree in the fence line seemed almost part of the tractor, I finally released the clutch. The tractor came to an immediate halt.

No harm done to the tractor, but it took several more weeks of coaching before I was allowed another solo driving effort.

13: IRONING

The iron was hot. Ma wet her finger and then touched the heat. I heard her finger sizzle. I thought for sure she would hurt herself, but she seemed not to mind at all.

Ma was tougher than my dad thought. He always said she needed protecting. From what? I wondered. She could touch a hot iron and not cry.

Sometimes the iron sat too long in one spot. It smelled sort of like leaves burning. Then I would hear Ma yell for sure. Shirts cost a lot in those days if you didn't have much to spend in the first place. Ma had a temper, all right. She was red-haired Irish and could scorch you if you got too close.

How those shirts smelled so fresh and new when Ma got it just right! They would crinkle. And if you hurried and put one on while it was still hot, it warmed you right down to your toes.

On good days, Ma spread her kind of sunshine to us all. She loved to play board games, cards and puzzles. When she laughed you knew things were okay; Ma didn't laugh enough.

14: THE KITCHEN TABLE

When I was a young child the kitchen table seemed to be the focal point of my world. Our kitchen was the typical large, old farmhouse kitchen. A wood-burning cookstove filled up one end of the room, a sink and cupboards stood along one wall, and a window in the other wall looked out onto a pasture. Opposite from the cookstove was the open archway leading to the rest of the house.

On cold winter mornings, the kitchen was the first place to which to run. The cookstove was already spewing forth warmth, and anything was better than the cold linoleum floor of the bedroom.

The kitchen table was where the family gathered for food preparation and for meals. This meant something was happening in the kitchen throughout most of the day. From the kitchen table I watched my mother cook. I smelled the odors of baking bread, boiling dill pickles, singed chicken feathers, and roasting beef. These odors often mixed with the more pungent, but not unpleasant kinds brought in from the barn. At that table, I often got the first taste of warm chocolate chip cookies, of blueberry pie, of homemade fudge or of buttered popcorn.

Often, Ma and I would try to surprise my dad and brother by popping lots of popcorn while they were in the barn milking, and then hiding it in the cupboards. Later, when I was old enough to work in the barn, I would enter the house on Saturday and Sunday nights and sniff the air. When Ma had made popcorn not only did the scent of freshly buttered popcorn give away her secret, so did the look on her face. While she tried not to smile, she never quite succeeded.

From the kitchen table my mother and I often shared the

excitement of watching the first snowfall of winter, and we each would try to be the first to spy the initial sign of spring: the return of the robin.

The kitchen table was a place for conversation. There, dreams were nurtured, triumphs celebrated, and disappointments shared.

The kitchen table was a gathering place for family and friends -- it wasn't until we got our first TV that the living room replaced the kitchen as the social gathering place. In the frigid cold of winter, the kitchen floor under the table was sometimes shared with a newborn lamb which had arrived earlier in the year than lambs were supposed to arrive. On that kitchen table, I played the boardgame *Uncle Wiggly* with my mother. My folks took days doing their taxes on that table.

The kitchen table was at the center of things for my farm family.

15: A HERD OF MY OWN

My family's dairy herd was almost entirely made up of Holsteins, but my dad often kept a Guernsey cow or two because, while they produced fewer gallons of milk, their butterfat production was much higher. When I was eight years old, a Guernsey cow gave birth to a scrawny female calf that my dad was not going to keep; the calf would go to market. She would not return much money, but we would have saved the cost of raising this calf that probably would never have much promise as a milker.

As a child, I did not recognize this economical argument. Instead, I pled with my father to save the life of the calf. "Give her to me," I said, "and I'll take care of her." My pleading went on for days until my dad gave in. After all, my older brother owned some hogs, and maybe this calf would help me learn more about being responsible.

I tended that calf like there had never been born a better calf. When she was two, we had a problem. I now "owned" a cow, but I would never be given any profit that she might earn because that was needed as part of the family income. By that time, I was ten, I wanted to join 4-H, and I needed a calf to show. With a little more pleading on my part I wrangled another deal with my dad. I traded him the Guernsey cow for a Holstein calf that I would show. I would keep any calves she might have in the future, and Dad would keep the milk. I named her "Rainbow."

When I was twelve, I bought my first purebred calf for a hundred dollars, which was a lot of money. A small portion of that money I had saved. The rest was a trade with my dad for some of the future calves that Rainbow might have. By the time I went to college, I had five head of Holsteins — that would have made a nice nucleus for a future herd.

Later, when the herd was sold, Rainbow, at the age of thirteen, was among them. Dad had held on to this special animal long after her milk production failed to cover the costs of upkeep. Rainbow had been the cornerstone of my 4-H experience and of my developing herd. She also had probably been part of my dad's dream of having one of his sons take over the farm. That dream was never realized.

16: GRANDPA

    Grandpa's image in the old black and white photograph is clear and strong. He looks to be a man in his fifties at the time the photo was taken.
    Initially one sees a balding man with a bushy moustache. His eyes appear gentle in contrast to that strong Roman nose characteristic of his English ancestry. While he does not seem to be a large man, his shoulders appear wide and able. His face shows lines etched by life's pains and filled in by the raw wind of the Kansas prairie which he loved.
    I know this man only through story. He died long before I was born. He had two sons. The younger one was my father.
    I grew up hearing very little about the man in the picture. The stories that were shared were filled with emotional conflict as my father's voice often choked when he spoke of his father. Head man of a threshing crew that worked its way during harvest from Oklahoma to North Dakota, Grandpa was often on the move.
    Yet there had been time to teach his son how to ride a horse, to share with him the love of the land, and to ground him in the values of work.
    And then when my dad was six, Grandpa left. He went back for a while to another wife and family in Missouri. Later when he returned to town, Grandma wouldn't let him live with her family, though she did permit my dad to go and work for him. It was good money for a hard working youngster.
    After Grandpa died, Grandma moved her family from Kansas to Iowa. And much later, my dad would marry and move to Illinois and then Wisconsin where I would hear the echoes of the past and wonder about this Grandpa of strength and industry.
    I wonder about who he was inside. Was he torn by loves

unvoiced? Love of different wives? Love of different children? Love of different self-identities? Who was he and how does he shape me now?

My parents said that I am the "spitting image" of my grandfather. These days when I look in a mirror, I can see they were right: Grandpa's face stares back at me.

My dad had but two possessions of his father: the Masonic shaving mug which used to sit on a shelf of mugs at the barbershop where Grandpa would go for a shave; and that old black and white picture.

I already have the shaving mug; I imagine the picture will come my way too. But is this all that I have of my Grandfather? I doubt it.

17: WORK HORSES

They were huge, with hooves large enough to do serious damage to any young boy or grown man who stepped too close or did not give proper warning when approaching. Even a thick muscled leg flicked quickly back to stretch a cramp or shake off a fly was cause for alarm.

Their names were Dolly and Molly, suggesting neither danger nor power. They were a matched set of Belgians: russet coats, four white socks, white manes and white tails. They were my dad's pride and joy. He bought them as yearlings and trained them himself to bridle and to harness.

We had an old Case steel-rimmed tractor that had to be hand cranked to start — Molly and Dolly were more reliable. A newer electric start *Case* was also used to work the fields, but when Dad wanted precision he always opted for the horses. They were used for planting corn, for cutting hay, and for pulling the windrower. When frigid cold temperatures made it difficult to start a tractor for hauling the manure out from the dairy barn, Molly and Dolly seemed pleased for exercise even when the snow was blowing sideways. They would also throw their massive heads about when they returned to the warmth of the barn, expecting and demanding more oats and more attention. Dad seldom let them down.

The horses were Dad's responsibility; rarely would he entrust their care to a son. Horses had been part of his roots growing up in western Kansas. They were his transportation to school and they made it possible for him to earn some money on nearby ranches.

Molly and Dolly, though, were not riding horses — they were work horses. They were kept, fed and cared for long after they were an economic asset to the farm. Tractors and self-propelled machinery eventually turned them into a luxury to be admired from a distance. Even then Dad would harness them up on occasion to give them a sense of purpose as well as to smell their sweat, to watch their flexing muscles, to listen to the thud of their hooves, and to appreciate the absence of roaring engines and motors.

My last vivid memory of Molly and Dolly came at the end of a long day of stone picking, hardly my favorite farm chore. My dad, my brother and I carried stone after stone from a swatch of the field to the stoneboat where we heaped them as high as we could. The horses were then asked to pull us and the stoneboat to a nearby fence line where we unloaded the stones and stacked them along the fence row. This mundane, monotonous cycle was repeated over and over until at last we had meandered up and down and across the field picking every rock that might pose a problem for the machinery which would be used to plant and harvest the field. By the end of the day, our muscles suffered from fatigue, but not those of Dolly and Molly. Stone picking was light work for them, requiring too much starting and stopping for their tastes.

On that afternoon of my last memory of these two huge creatures, we finished picking stone at the far end of the field. With a twinkle in his eye and giving a low chuckle, Dad turned to us and said, "Hold on tight. We're gonna give these two a chance to play." With that, I and my brother gripped the edge of the flat stoneboat and Dad braced his feet. Flipping the reins lightly he called out to Molly and Dolly, "Let's go now!" They lurched and he tapped their rears again with the reins urging them into a faster pace.

After that I lost track of what he was doing. I was just trying to hold on. We were flying across the furrowed ground kicking up as much dust as if we were at the back of a stampede. I pursed my lips tight and ducked my chin to my chest trying not to swallow, yet trying to breathe. I could still hear my dad calling to the horses, but couldn't tell what he was saying.

That ride seemed to go on forever. It was over too quickly. Dad tugged the horses to a halt at the gate. They blew air out their nostrils as if they needed to clear their windpipes too. They shook their manes and their skin quivered with anticipation as they waited to find out if they'd be allowed to run again or if they'd have go back to their stalls. I stood on shaky legs and brushed thick dirt from my clothes.

Dad turned back and grinned broadly at us. His teeth appeared strikingly white in contrast to the quarter inch of dust that covered his face and caked his eyebrows.

That was a rare moment for the horses and for us. Given the effort required to manage the farm, it was much more common to see my dad hard at work rather than hard at play.

Not long after that Molly and Dolly were sold to another farmer who still farmed the old way. We were moving on, embracing somewhat reluctantly the mechanized world. My dad did not want his dear friends to merely stand idly around day after day without purpose. Nor did he want to suffer the pain of watching them die.

After Molly and Dolly were sold, there were no more horses on our farm. There was no need for work horses no matter how good they might be. And there was no place for saddle horses on a dairy farm. That would be too frivolous.

What had been integral to our farm life — the neighing of horses when we pulled open the barn door — had first become nonessential and then a liability.

My dad grieved the loss of Molly and Dolly until his death.

18: GRADE SCHOOL TEACHER

The sun shines warmly as we ride our bikes down the hill a half mile to the four corners known as Punk. At the crossroads we turn right and pedal another half mile, across a creek, past a farm on the right and another on the left, both dairy farms. Cows graze. Two of them lift their heads in unison, curious at our passing.

Soon we arrive at our destination — a white, single room building. A woman stands at the door waving a hand in welcome. It is the first day of school. It is great to be back!

The school was my sanctuary. It was a relatively safe place. It was a window onto a world of imagination and dreams.

For me, school meant books, words, and images that expanded my mind and soul. School was Mrs. Staples — the teacher I had for six of my first eight grades. She was a woman who inspired, encouraged and stretched me beyond what I had believed possible. Through her I saw the possibility of a new and different world.

Mrs. Staples seemed old at the time. I expect she wasn't all that old. She played softball as hard as anyone and could hit a ball further than most. She had a two year teaching certificate. Not long after I entered high school, Mrs. Staples was told that she could no longer teach as her credentials did not measure up. Like the one room schoolhouse, she was no longer needed.

I saw Mrs. Staples once long after my formal education was completed. By then, I was a university professor — a path probably shaped by her more than any single other person in my life. She, this beacon onto the possibilities of life, was a clerk at a local store.

I had the opportunity to thank her for all she had done for

me. She had stayed informed about my career by talking with my parents from time to time. She inquired about what it felt like to walk daily across Harvard Yard and was pleased that I had not forgotten my rural roots. We reminisced about the old schoolhouse, books, and colorful memories. Mrs. Staples' eyes shone with pride when she spoke of her family and about her extended family — the many students she had taught.

Shortly thereafter, Mrs. Staples died. Her mind and spirit will not be forgotten by those of us she touched so deeply.

19: SUNDAY AFTERNOONS

Sunday afternoons were a time for rest on the farm. My parents often napped. Occasionally, we'd watch a football game on the TV. There were Sunday drives through the Kettle Moraine, or we might go to a farm in another community and pick up a calf that my dad had arranged to buy. When our herd was expanding fairly rapidly, we could not raise enough calves without purchasing newborns from other farmers. On many an occasion, my dad would drive the '51 Buick and he'd put the calf in the trunk, tie the lid down so there would be plenty of air, and drive very carefully home. Too often, the trunk was a smelly mess by the time we returned, but the calf was usually in good shape and happy to have a new home.

Before my brother started dating, he might take me along to an afternoon matinee or roller skating. In the summertime, we might walk back across our fields to the marsh and woods bordering our land. Or we might walk over to the gully where we dumped garbage and throw stones at tin cans. On very special Sunday afternoons, Dad would come out and hit flyballs to us in the open area of the orchard. We'd play 500, a game in which a catch of a flyball might count 100 points; a catch on the first bounce 50; and a roller 25. Whoever got to 500 first would take a turn at bat until another player reached the 500 score.

There was also a Sunday afternoon or two before hunting season when we would practice shooting tin cans with the shotguns. I was never very good at that. The barrel always seemed to weave and bob about, and then after several misses my eyes blurred with tears. My dad almost always hit the can. He'd hunted birds when he was a kid to help put meat on the table; he never lost that sharp eye. My brother was a fairly good shot too. As for me, my shoulder hurt from the kick of the gun, I couldn't see the tin can, and I wasn't positive I wanted to kill anything anyway. When I did kill a pheasant at the age of fourteen, I was torn between pride, grief, and guilt.

On most Sunday afternoons, particularly after my brother started dating, I spent much of my time in my room reading. Even though I likely picked up this habit in part from my parents, who also often spent some of Sunday afternoon reading, there were days when Ma and Dad threatened to kick me outside so I would do something other than read. At Christmastime I usually received three or four books. After one Christmas Day when by evening I had finished two books and started the third, I was restricted to reading no more than one book on that "family day." My love for reading can be easily traced back to Ma and Grandma who would spend a lot of time reading books to my brother and me. I always liked listening to the words as they painted a picture of a scene or person or an action behind my closed eyes.

There was a sense that summer afternoons could be "lazy and hazy." If it was really hot and humid, we might all sit under the chestnut trees and read or even play croquet while drinking homemade lemonade. That sense could change suddenly, though, if there was hay dry and ready to be baled and particularly if rain was in the forecast. And, of course, every Sunday afternoon ended when it came time for evening chores and milking.

20: HUNTER RABBIT

I am David in search of Goliath. I am Daniel Boone. Can you see my coonskin cap? I am primal hunter in search of prey.

Tip, my four-footed hunting companion, sniffs the air just above the bent grass. We move forward into a cavernous gravel pit. Here dragons could still roam. With pebbles in hand and on tiptoes, I and my dog move ever so slowly so as not to scare off any animal lurking about. Things seem the same as usual. Sand slides still in place. Three large rocks in the far corner. The old rusty, nearly forgotten manure spreader sits by the entrance on my right.

What's that?

At the bottom of a gravel slide some twenty feet away sits upright a rabbit with very tall ears. Tip stands solid still. My heartbeat quivers. Breath is hard to come by. I cannot believe my luck. Images of the hunt race through my mind. Undaunted by distractions, reason or common sense, I slip one pebble comfortably into my right palm. I desperately wish for a slingshot. None appears. Slowly, inch by inch, I raise my arm, cocking it like that pitcher for the Brooklyn Dodgers. With all the grace that a six year old boy can muster, I fling my deadly missile toward the neither bright nor swift rabbit.

No pitcher, no hunter was ever more accurate. The small stone clunks the rabbit on the head knocking him over like a bowling pin wiped out by a large round ball. Filled to overflowing with pride, I race to claim my prize.

The rabbit does not move. I grab him before Tip can.

By the ears I lift him above my waist so his feet do not touch the ground. Tip dances around me as I carry my game to the barn to show my parents.

Halfway there I look down at the dead rabbit only to have fantasies of Peter Cottontail scramble my head and heart. Will my parents really be pleased? Sure they will. I proved myself an able hunter.

Entering the barn, "Ma! Dad!" I holler. Both look up from spreading lime on the floor. "Look at what I got!" I yell, holding my prey as high as I can.

"What the hell!" Dad says.

"Oh, Bobby! What did you do?" Ma asks.

Just then the dead rabbit flings its body against the side of my head. Screaming, I drop him to the floor. Tip scrambles to get the rabbit. Dad calls him off.

The merely stunned rabbit makes his escape through the open doorway. Ma and Dad laugh so hard they cry. Me, I just cry.

21: MEASLES, CHICKEN POX, AND MUMPS

Some kids relished catching the flu or some other bug so they could stay home from school. I was not one of them.

Usually, I handled colds and flu well enough so I didn't miss much school. But chicken pox, mumps and two varieties of measles knocked me down over the course of three school years. I was out of school a week for each of them. In addition to these standard childhood diseases I had another problem in the fall of my tenth year which was more embarrassing and kept me away from school for weeks: ringworm.

I had had the habit of sitting in Rainbow's manger after my chores were finished. My calf would nestle her head on my lap and I'd scratch her behind the ears. In turn, she often licked my head until my cap fell off. That was how she transferred ringworm to my scalp. The only good thing about ringworm was that I did not have to stay in my room, but it took a long time before I could go anywhere without a bandage on a quarter of my head and before people decided I wasn't contagious.

Chicken pox, measles and mumps were more expected and acceptable diseases that struck most everyone in my age group. The first two to three days were the worst. That's when I had to stay in a darkened room. Later on, I was allowed to read. That made things a lot better, but I still couldn't go to school. My teacher, though, would drop off homework on her way home from school. That was particularly helpful when I was out so long with the ringworm. My mom would help me sort out the assignments and they would be passed back to the teacher when she stopped by with more homework.

Other than for the ringworm, there was no need to go to a doctor for illness. Mothers knew what to do for most ailments. There was always peppermint tea, Vicks vapor tents made of towels, ExLax, Castor Oil. Our entire school was transported to the Sullivan town hall to get smallpox shots. I received my polio shots and boosters in the doctor's office. I had a cousin who contracted polio; my parents were very determined about getting me those shots.

Once in a while the doctor would provide a pill. I was having stomach flu when the doctor came to the house to treat my mother for an ailment. He decided that he had a pill with him that would cure me, only it was twice the dose that I needed. The doctor took out a knife and cut the capsule in half. I could taste its contents all the way down; it was the most foul pill I've ever had. My stomach was indeed cured. I don't know if it was because the pill worked or because I refused to take another dose.

22: GRANDMA

I hold a photograph which at best is a fuzzy image of yourself. Yet there are strong bold features reflecting your journey.

As an eight year old girl, traveling by covered wagon from Central Iowa to western Kansas.

As a young woman, marrying a much older man — a crew boss on threshing crews that traveled long and far during harvest season. By necessity he was gone much of the time. Later, much later, you would learn of his other wife and family in Missouri. You weathered the divorce.

As a young mother of two boys, you met the family needs — physical, emotional and spiritual. You washed dishes at cafés and plucked feathers from chickens at a local produce house. Pride would not let you accept any "government dole." Your strength — outer and inner — carried you through.

As a middle aged woman, new strength was required and new tears wept when you buried your oldest son; he was only nineteen. How could you explain his death? He died from internal injuries caused by lifting the front-end of a Model T Ford to prove to his friends that he could do it.

You moved back and forth to Kansas and then Iowa again. There were more dishes; more chickens. You borrowed from relatives to purchase a tiny house across from the train yard in Clarion, Iowa. Years later, I loved to watch those great engines huff and puff, tug and pull moving a hundred or more cars. From this place you would not move. Tenacious. Through hip surgeries and life threatening ailments you remained a badger in your hole.

The picture I hold was taken when you were in your mid-

80s; you would live to be 96. In the fuzz of your image, there is the sure sign of stubbornness. You could intimidate easily — especially your daughter-in-law. Your way was the only way.

When I was little, we looked forward to you staying with us during the winter months; later, we came to dread those visits in the face of long winters. Tension increased in an already tense household — particularly between you and Ma. The playing cards had to be hidden. No Canasta while Grandma was with us! "Cards are the work of the Devil," you would say. Your stubbornness and rigidity cast, at times, a long constraining shadow over the family. Yet your life journey might have been impossible without the kind of determination and stubbornness you possessed.

Still, if we look deeply into the fuzz of your image, the playful child can be seen. There is the little girl, the woman, the mother, the grandmother who loved to tell stories, who enjoyed reading, who read books to us when we were young. You had so many stories of the West. There were stories of you as a young girl hearing of your parents seeing Kit Carson and you, yourself, seeing Wyatt Earp and Buffalo Bill pass through Kansas. Stories of the brother who helped build the Pike's Peak Railroad. And there were stories of relatives who were cattlemen, panners for gold, and even a Texas Ranger. Those stories drew me to the West like a magnet.

Your strength, your stubbornness, your playfulness, your stories remain part of me. Your image, your journey shape my own.

23: FERRIS WHEEL

I am a young child, probably somewhere between four and six years old. This is one of my earliest memories.

We are at a carnival. My brother and I and an older cousin go for a ride on a Ferris Wheel. My brother and cousin are eager to ride the Ferris Wheel and it is time for me to know the thrill of the carnival — so they say. After much coaxing, I hesitantly go with them to stand in line.

The huge wheel comes to a halt. People get off and we step forward to get on. I am helped into the seat. Herky-jerky, we are moved along as other people get into other seats. Our seat is rocking. My brother and cousin are laughing.

"Isn't this fun," they say.

I peek down through my legs. People look no larger than toy soldiers. My stomach leaps for my throat. My lungs can't get air; I can't breathe.

"I want out!" I scream. "Get me down from here."

The wheel lurches again. It feels like we are going to drop and then we climb higher. We stop at the very top while more passengers load.

I holler louder, "I want down!"

I try to lift the handle. It comes unlatched. My cousin grabs the handle and puts it back in place. I begin to crawl off the seat into the foot well.

Arms surround me and I am cussed at for being a scaredy-cat.

Now my brother is screaming at the man below to get us down. We are rocking back and forth for what seems like next to forever.

The wheel moves again. This time we move quickly, hurtling from the very top of the wheel to the bottom where we come to an abrupt stop. I am crying and throwing up.

The carnival man looms angry and threatening. "Why did you bring him on the ride?" he says accusingly to my brother and my cousin. To me he shouts, "You little cry baby, don't you ever come back here! Get the hell out of my way!"

My brother is angry; my cousin is angry.

I stand some three feet away with head down, sobbing. Everyone is angry with me. I am told not to tell my parents about the Ferris Wheel, "or else."

24: BELL RINGING

It is my day to ring the church bell. I don't often have that chance. Mr. Jenkins has gotten me out of Sunday School to assist him in announcing that it is nearly time for church.

He unties the rope from the wall and lets it hang. I can barely reach its frayed knotted end. I stand on my toes to manage a better grip. Mr. Jenkins nods and I pull.

At first there is only a clunk.

"Try again," Mr. Jenkins says. "You have to find the rhythm."

I nod, and pull again. I follow the rope downward with my upper body and then hold on tight as it takes its journey upward. Gradually, the clunking sounds become purer until I know I have it. Up and down I go until peals of the bell fill my ears.

Mr. Jenkins waves his arms for me to stop before the bell is damaged.

It is Sunday morning and I have called the people to God's house. I beam with pride as I join my family who are now taking their seats in a pew.

Now comes the hard part. Sitting through the church service is not always easy. I try to listen to the preacher, but sometimes I can't make sense of what he is saying. My folks say that, because our preachers are seminary students, a lot of people don't understand what they're talking about. But I am not supposed to squirm, yawn, or fall asleep — even though Mr. Nelson, sitting behind us, is already snoring and we've only sung one hymn.

I can read some of the words in the hymnal but not enough to sing along. It will be a good day when I can sing with everyone else.

I know the Lord's Prayer — at least that's something I can do. And I like it when the preacher tells us kids a story, but he doesn't do that very often. Someday I'll be like the older kids and go up to the pulpit to read from the Bible and that other reading stuff from the hymnal. It's kind of funny when Tommy Maxon gets up to read; he reads so fast no one knows what the scripture was about until the preacher explains it later. And Sally Dexter still has to stand on a stool to read. I wonder what would happen if she slipped and fell.

I like it when the preacher prays. No one is supposed to be watching me then, but I still get a squeeze on the arm from my mother most Sundays. I don't know why people look down to pray when God's supposed to be up there somewhere. It's surprising that Ma still has any strength in her fingers after scrubbing both my ears and my brother's. If clean ears make for good listening, then I ought to be a very good listener.

Yay! It's the last song. The preacher walks by and smiles at me. I, of course, smile back. He says his last words from the back of the church and we are done.

We fall in line to shake hands with the preacher. He sure has big hands — big feet too. My folks stop and talk with neighbors and I make a beeline for a friend.

She says, "The bell sounded real fine this morning, Bobby. I heard Mr. Jenkins say you did a good job. You must be getting strong."

I shove my hands in my pockets, nod, and look down to the gravel driveway to find a stone to throw.

25: TV COMES TO OUR HOUSE

Listening to the radio in the evening and on weekends was our family's entertainment in the late forties. My favorite programs were westerns: *Roy Rogers, Gene Autry, Lone Ranger, Bobby Benson and the B-Bar-B Riders,* and *Straight Arrow.* My parents liked *Tom Mix, Fibber Magee and Mollie, Mama,* and *the Shadow.* I didn't like *the Shadow* at all; it was far too scary. Unfortunately it came on right after the *Lone Ranger.* I tried hard to fall asleep on the davenport between "Hi-O Silver!" and the deep rumbling voice announcing *the Shadow.* Too often there weren't enough commercials and I was stuck with trying to go to sleep with dark and dangerous calamities taking place around the edges of my awareness.

An RCA Victrola that had to have seen better times was unpacked on special occasions and Ma and Dad would play their favorite records. The sounds were faded and scratchy, but they were sounds. My parents' love for music stemmed from their dating years when they'd go dancing. They still enjoyed going to dances when I was young — that was one skill that was not passed on to me.

One of the happiest days for my family in the late forties was the day we brought home a Philco Radio/Phonograph Console. The radio had much less static and the long-play records projected smooth, rich tones. We stayed up so late on that first night with the new phonograph that all of us, including my parents, fell asleep listening to records. My mother reports we didn't go to bed until three in the morning.

My music exposure was primarily the big bands of the thirties and forties, country western, and some pop music of the fifties that I listened to on my brother's car radio. Familiar tunes included *Tumbleweeds, Cool Clear Water, Dolly's Got a Hole in Her Stocking, Love Letters in the Sand, Que Sera Sera, Catch a Falling Star, Slow Boat to China, She'll Be Coming Around the Mountain,* and *Mule Train.*

I learned very little about Rock and Roll until I entered high school in the fall of 1958. I was aware of Elvis Presley and his song *Love Me Tender,* because one of the girls in our school sang it constantly. By that time, I also saw some of the Rock and Roll singers on the black and white TV but they had little impact on me. After I entered high school, I started listening to WLS from Chicago, but not before. I did not have my own radio until after 1958.

We got our first 12-inch black and white TV in 1951 and my world gradually changed. I could then put faces to characters that I had come to know from listening to the radio. But sometimes the TV images were not as good as my own.

Our introduction to the TV had come via Thursday night wrestling. For almost two years before purchasing our own set, we would join our neighbors in front of their tiny TV to watch wrestling. Actually, I played with our neighbor's daughter who was a year younger than me and was the closest to my ever having a sister. We would stop our playing and glance at the TV to see what all the fuss was about. After wrestling came the *Lucky Strike Hit Parade.* Once we got our own TV there was still an attempt to gather with our neighbors to watch some programs, but gradually that dropped off a lot.

The TV organized our evenings in ways that I don't remember the radio ever doing. It was easier to read a book with the radio on than with black and white images flittering across a screen. Programs we watched included the westerns we had listened to on the radio, *Ted Mack Amateur Hour, Texaco Star Theater with Milton Berle,* the *Ed Sullivan Show, One Man's Family, Father Knows Best, Ozzie and Harriet, I Love Lucy, Red Skelton, Martha Rae, Perry Mason, Kate Smith,* and *Big Top Circus* on Saturday mornings. There were brief news programs and of course there was Edward R. Murrow.

Sports made a splash on TV early. We watched boxing and football games. Much of this was before the Lombardi era with the Green Bay Packers. In those days, the Packers did so poorly that my parents rooted for the Cleveland Browns.

Work on the farm did not stop for Labor Day; Dad thought that was a day to work even harder. We did take a half day off on the 4th of July which was also my brother's birthday. We usually went to a nearby carnival and watched an American Legion ballgame. Other than milking, little work was done on Christmas or New Year's Day. The latter, once we had television, was a day for the Rose Parade and Rose Bowl. But work came to a halt for the baseball All Star game and as much as possible for the World Series. My folks rooted for the St. Louis Cardinals and for the Brooklyn Dodgers (or any other team for that matter) against the New York Yankees.

Of course, when the Braves moved from Boston to Milwaukee in 1953, we all became avid Braves fans, especially my mother. She hardly missed a game broadcast on the radio (it wasn't until much later that baseball games were routinely shown on TV). The *Milwaukee Sentinel* published player pictures and bios which my mother and I cut out and collected. And the local Milwaukee TV stations involved Braves players in so many ways in advertising and local game shows that not only were their names and faces known to us, we felt like they were neighbors.

Prior to the TV, we were exposed to cultures beyond our own through the movies. We would go to the movie theater four miles away or another one fourteen miles away. We seemed to do this as a family more often when I was quite young. Our movie adventures often revolved around westerns such as *Shane*, one of my parents' all time favorites, Tom Mix movies, as well as those with Lash LaRue, Roy Rogers, and Gene Autry. Jimmy Stewart, Doris Day, June Allison, Clark Gable, Debbie Reynolds were also favorites. Debbie Reynolds was the love of my young life. Seeing her in pigtails and blue-jeans was just about right.

Sometimes after a movie, we'd stop at the local drugstore for a banana split. And my all-time favorite was going to the A&W for a hamburger and root beer. The taste of those two items still remains buried somewhere in my taste buds. On very special summer evenings after milking we would make the trip to the A&W — no movie was even needed to make that an enjoyable evening.

Those trips to town, along with those to neighbors, didn't occur as frequently after the arrival of that tiny black and white TV. There were programs to be watched and not missed. Since many of the programs my folks liked didn't particularly interest me, I eventually learned how to read a book in front of the TV. With the advent of the TV, it seemed like more time was spent paying attention to people hundreds and thousands of miles away and less time to those nearby.

26: COW TANK

Come with me for a moment and look at the water in the cow tank on the east end of the barn. The tank is about eight feet long, thirty inches wide and three feet tall. It is made of aluminum and has a bar stretching across its middle.

Islands of algae float on the water's surface. Tiny green and brown bugs flit about. One wonders how many of these will wind up in a cow's nose or stomach.

Water enters the tank when the wooden float sinks far enough to pull tight the chain attached to it, in turn opening the shutter on the pipe.

The tank is cleaned perhaps three or four times a year. It is scrubbed with a steel brush; then it sparkles, as if new. Then, the water appears fresh, but not now; not this evening. It has been a long time since cleaning. Reflecting many shades of greens, browns and blues, the water is less than inviting.

I am eight years old playing outside the barn, well away from the tank's murky depths. My dad is in the barn milking the cows. I imagine that I am a baseball player and hit some home runs with a stick and pebbles. I imagine I am an airplane floating in the sky, then dive bombing. I make small circles with my feet, then larger ones, then smaller ones again. Slowly I revolve and then faster, spinning. Eyes closed. Arms wide spread and then reaching for the sky. I am free, dizzy, spinning like a top crashing, splashing into the cow tank.

The shock. I can't see. I can't breathe. Taking in putrid water. I gag. I lurch up and hit my head on the crossbar. Down again. I heave upward. Again the crossbar. No air. Only water and panic. I believe I'm going to die. Light, loss, fright. "Help!" I scream in my head. No one hears. Not much time. Yet again I try to get my head above the water's grasp. This time I avoid the crossbar. Air enters my lungs with a blast as greenish water spews from my throat. I rest a minute with my head and shoulders draped over the tank. Then I drag my body out. I am crying. I am tired. I am ashamed for doing such a stupid thing.

Drenched and smelly I enter the barn to tell my dad. I know he will not understand. I will now be dried by the heat of his anger.

27: CHESTNUT TREES

Two chestnut trees stood side by side in our front yard. Huge in size, they offered a canopied shelter to keep me dry during a rainstorm, or a darkened shade to keep me cool on a sweltering day. The ground at the base of the trees was bare dirt from lack of sunshine.

In late springtime, chestnut flowers — red and white — sprinkled the ground. Their sweet perfume attracted bumble bees. The droning of those many yellow-black shells that flew efficiently gathering nectar was almost deafening. "Don't go near the chestnut trees," Ma said. "Bumble bees sent Danny Johnson to the hospital just last week."

In the summer the ripening chestnuts grew in green hulks. These made great baseballs. I hit them with a stick. Sometimes their casings would fly off. Depending upon the distance a chestnut flew, it was counted as a single, double, triple or homerun. Given the size of the chestnut and of the stick, there were more strike outs than I liked.

In the fall, the chestnuts freed from their hulls glistened mahogany-brown. These made even better baseballs, but were a nuisance to be gathered up with the leaves.

In the winter, the chestnut trees stood nude before the wind seeming cold, yet strong. They stood as vivid dark reminders of warmer days and of nature's promise for a coming season of renewed growth and opportunity.

28: COUNTY FAIR

There is a picture of me at the age of ten with my black and white Holstein calf, named Rainbow. In one hand, I hold the lead rope attached to the halter making sure Rainbow does not decide to walk out of the picture. In the other hand, I am holding a blue ribbon. I am beaming proudly.

The Jefferson County Fair was the highlight of summer. As did the other boys and girls showing calves, I worked all spring preparing Rainbow for the show. A young calf does not naturally want to be led, prompted to stand, and wait for the judge's eye to evaluate her conformation and ability. A ten-year old boy does not naturally know how to gentle a calf, how to work with a calf as a team member, or how to be satisfied with imperfections in ability or form. We taught each other, Rainbow and I. We learned from each other — sometimes the hard way.

In those early days of teaching and learning, Rainbow dragged me from the garden through the cowyard. Stubbornly, I would not let go of the lead rope. Eventually she would tire and I'd pick myself up, brush off my clothes, and start leading her again. The biggest bruise was to my ego.

My brother said, "You need to hit her upside the head. Teach her who's boss."

I didn't. Rainbow and I were good friends sorting out a relationship.

Over time, she learned to be led quite well and I learned to show her with a satisfactory level of skill. We worked together daily. I would brush her, trim her feet, and clip her hair. She received more baths than she probably should have. Then there was the walking and standing just right. Rainbow had push button controls buried in her front left shoulder. I could push one way on a cord within that shoulder and her back left foot would move, making her stand square and correct. Or, perhaps, the right hind foot needed to be moved in a similar fashion. The controls were hidden there in her shoulder. Together, we learned to operate them.

And then to the county fair we went.

"Don't be disappointed with whatever you get," Dad counseled. "This is your first time. It's your calf's first time. Pay attention and learn what you can."

When Rainbow and I entered the show ring, I had no idea there would be a total of fifty calves being shown by 4-H kids from ten to eighteen years old. It took the judge a long time to evaluate each calf and to compare them to each other. We had walked around the ring several times and the judge had come by to look at Rainbow, as he had with each calf. At last he motioned for us to line up in the order that he selected. Rainbow and I weren't at the front of the line, but we were closer to the front than the back. No one had explained to me how ribbons were distributed. With such a large class, ten calves received blue ribbons, ten red ribbons and so on. I was shocked when I was handed the last blue ribbon! Trying not to beam too much, I led Rainbow out of the ring to show the ribbon to my parents. In addition to the blue ribbon, I had also received a two dollar bill from the Holstein-Friesian Association. I had never seen a two dollar bill before.

As a member of the Oak Hill Hustlers 4-H Club, I was one of several boys and girls responsible for maintaining our area in the pole barn where our cattle were tied side by side. We maintained that area with great care and had much pride in our green and white 4-H sign proclaiming to all those city folk who we were.

My memories of the county fair are lodged in my mind's eye, in my muscles, in my nostrils — perhaps more than anywhere, in my nostrils. The smells were rich and earthy. There was, of course, the cow manure which we escorted to the manure pile as soon as it hit the floor. The smells of manure co-mingled with those of fresh straw, new alfalfa hay, shampoo, soaps, talcum powder, peroxide and oils. These latter were used to keep white, white and black, black. And smells of freshly cleaned leather halters merged with those of hot mixed mash.

The dirt walkway behind our calves was raked clean on an hourly basis. At least two of us were on duty throughout the day.

Sounds of the midway filtered into the barn. We usually arrived on Thursday, and by Saturday afternoon were ready to explore the midway to discover what all the noise was about. There were shouts of peddlers peddling flame eaters, kewpie dolls, and mysterious women who would come out to twirl tassels in strong, suggestive ways. Screams of girls on the Tilt-a-Whirl, the Octopus, and the Rocket Plane greeted us as we walked the midway. It didn't take long to run out of time, money or interest.

But the county fair, then and now, had little to do with the midway. It was all about a young boy and a young calf learning from and teaching each other.

29: THE LIBRARY

My eyeballs threatened to jump from their sockets. My breath was caught somewhere deep in my belly. I had never seen anything like it. My head swiveled up and down, left and right. Bight colors, dull colors looked back at me. Row after row stacked upon one another. The single-room building in whose doorway I stood was ringed with books, books and more books. Small books, large books, thin books, fat books. In my entire eleven years I had never seen so many books.

"Can I help you, young man?" The kindly voice came from a gray-haired lady sitting behind a very large desk. On the desk were a number of long boxes. Some were wooden and some cardboard. I was to learn that each box held cards with information about a book — these cards could tell a person where to find any book in the room.

"I would like to borrow a book, please," I whispered.

"Oh, you can borrow more than one if you like."

"Really!" I nearly shouted. "Boy." My eyes darted from wall to wall trying to take in each book.

"Did you have a particular book in mind?"

"No."

"Well, what kind of book might you be interested in? Sports? History? Westerns?"

"Westerns, I think."

"Very well." Getting up from her chair, the woman walked to the wall on my right. "Our Westerns are in this section. Look at as many as you like. You may borrow up to ten books at once for two weeks. If you bring them back late, though, you will have to pay two pennies a day as a fine. You won't be late will you?"

"No, Ma'am."

I studied those books something fierce. I wanted my first books from a library to be the right ones. Several books were stacked in my arms as I left that cave of volumes and a new library card, which the helpful librarian had shown me how to fill out, was buried deep in my back pocket. Zane Grey's *Wildfire* and *Riders of the Purple Sage* were among the books that I had borrowed, as was a book that inspired my own dreams of writing more than I may even now realize. The book was entitled *The Outlaws of the West*. It was written by Robert M. Coates.

Proudly, I walked back to the old green Buick, parked in front of the barbershop, where my folks waited.

30: CHOPPING ICE

After checking my ear lappers to be sure no more skin is exposed than has to be and zipping up my heavy coat, I heft a maul, reach for a shovel, grab the water hose, and head out the barn door to check on the condition of the water tank. I hunker down against the wind and walk the hundred yards or so to the tank.

On this bitterly cold January morning, I find the surface of the stainless steel tank frozen solid. I lift the maul and let it fall of its own weight; it simply bounces off the ice. Standing back from the tank so I won't be splashed with frigid water, I swing the maul with full force. A jagged fissure runs the length of the tank. Three more swings of the maul and I break through six inches of thickness. The force of the maul carries its head and much of its handle toward the bottom of the tank. Quickly, I jerk it out; water dripping from the steel head never reaches the ground as ice immediately encrusts the maul nearly up to my gloved hands. I then shovel the chunks of ice out onto the ground so the tank won't immediately freeze over. Once I refill the tank, I drain the hose and return to the warmth of the barn, wondering how the heifers can stand drinking such cold water and knowing that within four hours I will go back out and break a new hole in the ice so they can drink again.

Winter in southern Wisconsin was potentially dangerous for cattle and those who took care of them. Milk cows were only permitted outside briefly on cold days for exercise, and when the thermometer dropped below zero they remained in their stanchions. Hogs rarely ventured out on such days even though they had access. And the heifers, pastured outside, sought refuge from the wind in open sheds.

Cold or not, these animals had to be looked after. They required fresh water, feed and bedding. Much of my time in the winter, along with my dad's and brother's, was seeing to these basic needs. There were days when the snow drifted as high as the roof on the farrowing shed. At other times six-foot long icicles, ten inches around, hung from eaves — they were at once beautiful creations inspiring wonder, and potentially deadly objects for both animals and humans.

The barn had to be cleaned even on days when snow blew crossways making visibility nearly impossible. Those were the mornings in my younger days when my dad preferred to use the work horses to pull the manure spreader. "Horses know the way back to their stalls," he explained. "A tractor don't."

The barn never felt better than on these cold mornings with snow blowing about. Huddled against the wind and that first burst of cold, it took a lot of effort for us to forge through the snow from the house to the barn. Once inside though, we were greeted with enough warmth that we removed our heavy coats and gloves.

Usually, a few cows would acknowledge our arrival with stares and soft lowing. Those more impatient for feed or to be milked tossed their heads about. We often stood inside the closed door for a moment and breathed deeply the odors of hay, straw, silage, manure, lime, and cows, knowing that here in this barn we were needed, and that there was purpose to everything we did — even chopping six inches of ice in a cow tank, rather than remaining snuggled deep in a warm bed.

31: WINTER DREAMS

The work pace slowed quite a bit during the winter months. Cows still had to be milked twice a day and it took longer to do the routine barn chores, but depending on the weather, there was time during the late morning and early afternoon to go shopping, to read, or to dream.

Winter was a time for our family to dream. There seemed always to be a new scheme for expanding or improving our base of operation, for considering an alternative cash crop, or for thinking about an entirely different enterprise. One winter my parents decided to raise pickles as a cash crop; the nearby pickle factory made marketing convenient. They planted an acre of cucumbers. Fortunately, I wasn't old enough to pick pickles, but Dad, Ma, and my brother picked them until they had a hard time standing back up. There was even a day when a vacuum cleaner salesman came by and was told that my dad and Ma would listen to his spiel if he'd first spend an hour picking pickles. My folks never had to sit through the man's sales pitch. Raising pickles was a one year venture.

Then there was the winter when we all got excited about raising worms. After all, people from Illinois were driving by our place to go fishing every day in the summer. We sent off for information, worm bedding and worm feed. My dad and brother constructed several worm boxes in which the worms would be nurtured and raised. By the time spring came along, my dad was busy in the fields and the worm boxes remained empty. I used some of them for storing products for my pretend grocery store.

One of the most serious winter dreams was turning the gravel pit into an active pit. My brother was particularly excited about this plan because he wanted to drive trucks and Caterpillars. This dream took more than one winter to consider. We actually went to Milwaukee and looked at cats, trucks and backhoes. My brother got information on training to become a large machine operator. But the entire gravel trucking idea eventually fizzled largely, I imagine, for lack of investment resources.

Winter was the time of year when we decided to raise Landrace hogs, thought about constructing a new corn crib, made plans for expanding the dairy herd, weighed the advantages of switching from storing milk in a can cooler to a bulk milk cooler which we never bought, and considered the potential for buying a second farm.

It may be that winter dreaming was a way of dealing with winter doldrums and with the inevitable dreaded tax season. The latter would often take weeks of afternoons to complete. My folks had designated card tables to hold various stacks of bills and receipts as well as a hand cranked adding machine. Those were often afternoons when as a child you stayed out of the way.

In any case, winter dreaming provided for a fair amount of family interaction. Sometimes it led to disappointment; other times it led to new opportunities taken. In the beginning, my folks had followed their dream of being farmers. That dream was reshaped from time to time to fit the realities of the situation, but it was a dream they realized. And they taught us kids, through winter dreaming, never to accept the status quo as what has to be.

Dream, weigh the risks, and act.

32: SCHOOLYARD BULLIES

From the first day of school, it did not take long to learn to stay away from schoolyard bullies. I discovered quickly that there were at least two pecking orders in a one room school.
The first was measured by the ability to intimidate. The second had to do with smarts in the classroom. Seldom was there much correlation between the two pecking orders, but it proved necessary to manage both.
I handled the bullies primarily by avoidance, and for the first two years, by also having an older brother in the upper grades who would defend me from time to time. For the most part, I tried to avoid confrontation. Still, I had to withstand threats, teasing, and occasional bodily attacks sometimes disguised as "touch football" or "accidentally running me over during a game of tag" or some other group activity. Most of the bullies were boys. While I was in the first and second grades, there were older girls who enjoyed playing "boys against the girls" (a game in which one side would capture the other). Several times after capturing me these older girls would get me on the ground and try to kiss me. I would squirm and kick to get away from them, sometimes with success. When I was older, I always wondered where those girls went.
Eventually, I moved up the scale of toughness. By the third and fourth grade I had learned the art of standing up for myself. Often, that meant simply refusing to display any sign of fear or pain. Sometimes, it meant being able to run faster than most of the others. And on occasion, I got in my own licks.
One of those times took place toward the end of the noon hour recess. We were playing touch football. The teacher

had announced that the offense would have one more series of downs, giving them the opportunity to tie the game. I was playing defense. Three pass attempts failed. On fourth down, their passer connected with the school's number one bully — an eighth grader who had been held back twice. With a broad grin on his face he ran toward my right. I sped to meet him and threw a perfect flying block — just like the one I had seen pictured in the school encyclopedia. The impact of my body, although much smaller than his, crumpled his legs. He hit the ground hard and fumbled the ball. Kids on both sides applauded and chattered about the daring play. Embarrassed and enraged, my adversary lunged for me; but the teacher stepped between us and declared the game over.

As I moved into the higher grades, it was no longer okay to run from a fight. I had to stand up for myself. I didn't have very many fights, though — it seemed that once you had proven yourself there were fewer challenges.

But there was one memorable fight when I was in the sixth grade. It started toward the end of the noon hour after the teacher had gone inside to set up the classroom. There was no victor by the time she rang the bell to call us in. While the teacher was working with a class in the front of the room, my opponent, an eighth grader, let it be known through whispers relayed from student to student what he was going to do to me if I dared to go outside for the afternoon recess.

Of course, I had no choice. We wrestled and clawed at each other for another ten minutes or so surrounded by a ring of boys and girls, but again there was no clear victor at the end of recess.

After school we bumped into each other on the porch, grudgingly nodded, and then raced for our bikes to pedal home. There were farm chores to do and neither one of us wanted to risk angering our fathers by being late.

33: GROWING THE HERD

In the late forties, our milking herd of Holsteins was modest, ranging between twenty-five and thirty milking cows plus heifers and calves. In addition to a stanchion for each cow, there were two box stalls that were used for cows ready to deliver or for young calves still being fed milk by hand with a pail. This was one of my first chores and one that I enjoyed a lot, but it was not without peril.

A calf might be allowed to suckle its mother for three days or so until the cow no longer produced the overly rich colostrum — good for newborn calves but not for humans. Once the cow's milk was fit for human consumption, her milk went into the milk cans and off to market. Her calf received milk into which a mix of nutrients had been stirred.

Calves knew how to suckle, but they had to learn how to drink from a pail. To teach them, I would straddle the calf's neck facing its head, frequently backing it into a corner so it would have less freedom to move about. Once in position, I'd hold a bucket with some milk in it beneath the calf's nose and gently push its head until its nose broke the surface of the milk. Sometimes as the calf sought air it would open its mouth and take in milk and learn quickly how to drink. Others, more often than not, required more assistance. For those, I'd place my finger into the calf's mouth which the calf would begin to suck. Then, I'd lower my hand and the calf's mouth into the milk. The calf would take in milk while suckling my finger. It might take several mornings and evenings before the calf grasped how to drink so I could remove my finger.

There was plenty of room for error in this process. The calf could buck its head and try to escape. More than once, sharp newborn teeth sliced my finger. And even after the calf knew how to drink, it could become impatient with how slowly it was getting milk and butt the pail out of my hands. Lost milk was lost profit and not welcomed.

At the other end of the barn were four horse stalls. Two were used for horses. The other two housed the lime that was used to help sanitize the barn floor each day as well as various feed mixes, such as molasses and the mix put in the calves' milk.

At that time each cow had its name printed in red paint on a gray piece of aluminum that hung over its stanchion. There was Boss, Betsy, Blackie, Nancy, Hazel, Lady, Mabel, and Kicker to name a few. Kicker was a cow that required a lot of caution. I never did milk her.

The herd grew just as my brother and I grew. The first major change was moving the workhorses out of the barn and into a shed. The four former horse stalls were torn out and replaced with stanchions for more cows.

Next, perhaps the most symbolic of changes, was the removal of the name signs from over the stanchions. We were now milking more cows than could come into the barn at once. The name signs were replaced by chains and numbers that hung around the cows' necks. I complained to my dad about that change. It didn't feel right not having a name for a cow. He agreed, sadly. Dad was close to many of his cows. When Blackie, one of his foundation cows, finally had to go to the stockyard, Dad cried. I only saw him cry twice before I was old enough to leave the farm. The second time was when his closest friend died.

So Dad agreed that we were taking a step backward while taking a necessary step forward. We had to produce more milk and that meant diminishing the personal relationship we had with our animals. It was about this time, when I was twelve, that he gave me the task of managing the breeding program for our herd. That meant that I kept a record of heats, breedings, and calvings, and I made recommendations regarding the bulls to request when the artificial inseminator arrived. From that point on, at least during the summers and weekends, I took care of meeting the inseminator and being responsible for getting the cow back to the herd. I imagine one reason Dad gave me this responsibility was that I could put names down on the charts for each cow whether there was a nameplate above the stanchion or not.

I never took to machinery or machine repair like my brother did, but if my dad and brother had to work late in the field or on repairing machinery, I handled the cows and started the milking. Cows needed to be milked at a given time twice a day; they did not want to wait for a field to be plowed or for a combine to be repaired.

The herd had definitely grown. We were now producing over twenty-one ten-gallon cans of milk a day.

By the time I graduated from grade school, we had bought a second farm across the road. That eventually took the strain off the barn at the home farm, because we split the herd in two.

But the nameplates never returned.

34: WEIGHING MUSICAL SCALES

My musical career was brief by anyone's standard. It was Ma's idea that I learn to play a musical instrument. She had played a piano some, but we didn't own one of those and there was little space to add it in our house.

The accordion was the alternative. It was a fairly popular instrument in southern Wisconsin in the fifties. Polka bands were everywhere. And of course Lawrence Welk made the accordion popular on black and white TV.

I was an interested student, if not eager. We had to travel fourteen miles to a neighboring town for lessons. That meant my dad drove me, because Ma never learned how to drive. We usually went after the cows had been milked, so it was fairly late when I met with the music teacher. Saturday lessons were better, but that meant Dad would have to leave whatever he was doing to take me.

Finishing the basic paperwork assignments — distinguishing among notes, bars, chords and so on — was not difficult. Some of those we had learned during our general music lessons in grade school. Practice was another matter. I would practice in my room for a half hour after supper before going out to the barn. My dad and brother tried to leave the house before I started. Ma closed the door to my room. I'm not sure I ever had an ear for music. But some of what I produced on the accordion was deafening. Strident might be a more appropriate word for it.

After six months of lessons and practice, I did improve. There were small recitals during evening school programs where I played *Row, Row Your Boat* and *She'll Be Comin' Round the Mountain*. Although the audience applauded, I did not enjoy being in front of people. I was always afraid that my sheet music would flutter to the floor and that I'd freeze before the stares of our neighbors.

It was at this juncture in my musical career that a huge decision was thrust upon me. I had progressed through the beginner's accordion that we had rented from the music store where I took lessons, and I was now ready to advance to intermediate music. That meant that it was time to purchase a full-sized accordion, and that was going to be a sizeable investment.

Spring was rapidly approaching. The Milwaukee Braves had already gone south to start their spring training. My mind was on baseball. Daily, I'd study the section of the Sears catalog that offered baseball gloves for sale. Purposely, I'd leave it open for my folks to find. Hint! Hint!

Eventually, Dad asked what I'd prefer: a full-sized accordion, or the baseball glove. That was like dangling fresh meat before a half starved dog. The baseball glove, of course, won the day. There was never a doubt.

Ma was not pleased with this decision, but acquiesced — I'm sure in part because of the cost of the accordion and additional lessons.

I made two additional tentative forays into the music world. By the time I was in the sixth grade, I loved to sing. I would sing with a full voice from deep within the diaphragm, and I swayed with the rhythm of the tunes. I'd sing to the cows during milking and I particularly enjoyed singing carols during the school Christmas program. Until, that is, some of the older boys laughed at my moving to the music. The teacher told them to stop, that I was letting my body feel the music and that was good. But the damage had already been done. I never liked being laughed at. From then on, I stood rigidly to sing and I held in my voice until I was convinced that I could not sing.

Ma made one additional valiant attempt to get me involved in music. When I was twelve, I was old enough to hunt and it was time to get my own shotgun. That was a long awaited rite of passage for a boy raised in the country. Ma said she'd go along with my getting a gun if I agreed to take band when I entered high school. Naturally, I agreed. But no one remembered by the time I went to high school.

One of my few regrets in life is that I never developed whatever innate musical talent I might have had. Ma tried. But it was a definite challenge to arrange and pay for music lessons and instruments when the family had to respond to the rhythms of the seasons and the demands of the land.

35: IN THE STARS

There were no sharp edges delineating boundaries between farm, school and church in our rural community. Any intended lines were blurred. I expect the resulting fuzziness had a lot to do with our give-and-take relationship with the land.

That relationship was as personal as those with family members, neighbors and animals. The first corn plant poking its green leaves through the soil prompted a sense of awe and faith in knowing that after a harsh winter, the land remained productive, capable of nurturing new life. We watched that corn grow tall, eventually towering over our heads, and we began to imagine a bountiful harvest. And then the hail would come and we'd pray that the corn would survive. Or there might be a summer without timely rainfall and again we'd worry whether there would be enough corn to feed the cattle. After a good growing season, when the silos and corn cribs were filled, we knew the satisfaction of having successfully partnered with the land. The ground would lie fallow for the winter renewing itself; we trusted that beneath four-foot snowdrifts nature was preparing for yet another season.

The revolving seasons shaped the land and our lives. That seasonal clock was more important than any alarm clock would ever be. It not only marked subtle and then dramatic changes in the landscape, it made very clear that we only worked with the land — we were never in complete control. There were patterns and powers beyond reach. Thus the land took on a sacred quality and directed us toward the holy.

The land contained mystery, as did much that took place on the farm. When I was old enough to do chores in the barn but not yet able to milk cows, after finishing filling water tanks and putting hay in the mangers, I'd follow my dad from cow to cow as he milked, asking question after question. He must have been a fairly patient man because he seldom turned me or my questions away.

Often we talked about the mysteries that surrounded us. The thrills of helping a cow deliver a calf. Why cows have four stomachs and how they work. Why we rotated our crops to better care for the land. How corn pollinates. How manure replenishes the soil. Why sows may have fourteen pigs and cows usually have but one calf. Why some cows, for example Jerseys, produce milk with higher butterfat content than others such as Holsteins.

Walking from the barn to the house after finishing milking often took much longer than it should have. We'd stop along the way to stare up at the bright stars against an inky sky and Dad would point out constellations that his mother had pointed out to him when he was young. Or we'd talk of the universe and wonder about how that sky stayed so much the same, even though it appeared different from hour to hour and season to season.

We didn't often speak explicitly of God, but the whispered sense of awe, of being part of something much bigger than ourselves, of being stewards of things almost holy, permeated how we thought about and how we walked upon the land.

36: GEESE FLY NORTH

I watch eight Canadian geese in a low tight vee hunkered against the western sky steadily winging their way northward. Beams of the rising sun bounce off their dark wings and white bellies.

Entranced, I stop, set down the buckets of slop I am carrying to the hog shed and wait for the small flock to pass by. There will be much larger flocks coming soon. This one is a sign of spring and the change of seasons. These geese are not to be missed.

I wave at them. They honk. They are so close that it seems like I can see their eyes watching me.

Time freezes for a moment. They are huge. They are majestic. They urge me to think of what lies over the horizon.

I wish I could fly, that I could follow them.

I watch until I hear them no more. They become specks against white billowy clouds. Then they are gone.

"Get your mind on your job!" Dad hollers from the barn doorway. "We don't have all day to feed those hogs."

Without looking back, I pick up the buckets of slop and trudge to the hog pens wondering what those geese will see before the day ends and where they will sleep tonight.

37: BIRTH AT TWENTY BELOW

It was a frigid February morning at about 2:00 a.m. when Dad woke me. Rebecca was ready to have her babies. Rebecca was my first hog, a very large white Landrace sow I had bought with my own money. I was eleven. Dad knew I didn't want to miss out on the birthing.

We bundled up in heavy clothes, tucked our heads down to brace ourselves against the bite of the wind, and slowly made our way to the stone-bottomed building which had been turned into a farrowing shed. Once inside we took off our outer coats — the building was toasty warm. Thick walls provided shelter from the wind, and six separate heating lamps beamed warmth for new born pigs.

Six farrowing stalls were available. Each stretched some fifteen feet in length and was about three feet wide, just wide enough for the sow to turn around. At one end of each stall there was a three by three foot section separated by a slatted gate under which the little pigs could travel to seek safety from the sow, and over this safety zone hung the heat lamp.

On this particular morning, two of the farrowing stalls were already filled with sows and their respective litters. In the four other pens lay four more sows awaiting their time for birthing. Rebecca was in the farthest stall. Her water had already broken. We knelt beside the pen and waited.

The first pig arrived less than half an hour after we settled in. I immediately picked him up, toweled him off and placed him under the heat lamp to dry. It is dangerous for newborn pigs to be left with their mother while she is birthing, since she often gets up and down and flops around indiscriminately. Clearly, our presence was very much needed, and I was awestruck to be participating in this event. The next two pigs came rather quickly. Sometimes a sow's cough would produce a pig.

Then Rebecca stopped. Certainly she would have more than three pigs — Landrace were noted for having large litters, and fourteen or sixteen pigs were not uncommon.

Her labor picked up again. She strained, but no pig came out. She strained again and still no pig. She stopped straining. I did not know what was happening. I glanced over at my dad who was frowning.

We waited anxiously a few more minutes. Rebecca made no effort to move or resume her contractions.

Dad nodded at me and said, "Looks like she's got a problem. Likely the next pig is twisted."

"What can we do?" I asked.

"We could call Doc Henry." Dad scowled. "But it would take a couple hours for him to get here. By that time we would probably lose the rest of her pigs." And he added softly, with his eyes averted toward the sow, "We could also lose Rebecca."

Fighting back tears, I couldn't get a word out. Silently, I urged my dad to come up with a solution.

"We need to go inside her and try to help Rebecca," he offered. "The pig that's sideways has to be straightened out in the birth canal."

I nodded, sort of understanding.

"Doc would use forceps." Dad looked at me. "You have the smallest hands and wrists. I might hurt her with my large hands. You could get the job done with the least amount of damage. Are you willing to try?"

I nodded my head up and down, not knowing what I was really agreeing to. But with Dad as coach, I climbed into the stall and positioned myself behind Rebecca. He told me to place my fingers carefully in the birth canal. Trying hard to ignore the blood and other oozing fluids as well as the smells, I did as I was instructed.

"Push in further," Dad said.

Closing my eyes, I pushed.

"Do you feel anything?"

"Only water," I replied.

"Push further."

I did. I was nearly up to my right elbow. My fingers suddenly bumped into something hard and warm. "I feel something." I said. I wiggled my fingers until I could get them around the piglet. "I've got it."

"Good. Try to find the head end and turn the pig so it's facing you."

Without too much effort I had the pig turned. I nodded and whispered, "OK."

"Now back your hand out and Rebecca will do the rest."

As I cleaned off my hand and arm with straw, Dad said quietly, "You did a good job, Bobby. Most often the twisted pig comes out dead. Be prepared."

We waited. No more than five minutes passed before the pig that had blocked the channel popped out; she was alive. I picked her up, wiped her off and placed her with her brother and sisters under the heat lamp. The rest of the birthing went well without further complication.

Within an hour and a half, Rebecca delivered eleven more healthy pigs.

To be part of this creative process was awe-inspiring. There would be many more births of pigs and calves where I would assist. None, however, would surpass the satisfaction of that February morning when I took my place among the midwives of history.

I would also witness much death on the farm, yet after that morning, death could only take its natural place beside birth. It could not overpower hope, newness and creation.

38: SHOW AND TELL

As a young lad on a farm, I thought I knew something about sex. I had witnessed hogs doing it as the sow raced across the enclosed pasture dragging the boar behind. Cats, too. The cows didn't help much since they were artificially inseminated; still, I watched the inseminator do his work with more than idle interest.

"I'll trade you my Oreo cookie for your pickle," the girl with the big lips said. At twelve, Alice was a woman of the world. I was eleven and had admired her growing humps for over a year. Alice was a tease with most of the older boys, but she seldom had much to say to me.

She had knelt in front of me to make her request. I was sitting on the ground with my back to a tree eating lunch; home plate was just behind us some thirty feet away. Not far away was the boys' outhouse. If the wind came from the wrong direction you would know it was there before you saw it.

Not having a very good day, I had sought to be alone with my lunch. The other kids were scattered in twos and threes across the schoolhouse porch and under the trees which ringed the driveway. I had been alone until Alice made her request.

Her short navy blue skirt was hiked to mid-thigh; her thin red sweater tightly shielded those mysterious mounds. I remembered seeing pictures of naked breasts in my brother's room.

Embarrassed by my own thoughts, I responded hesitantly, "Sure." I wasn't overly fond of pickles anyway. "Thanks," I added as I gave her my pickle wrapped in plastic wrapping paper. She grabbed the pickle, squeezing it and my hand while depositing the Oreo in my palm.

Grinning she said, "You're cute when you blush. You want to see my panties?" Without waiting for a response, she raised her skirt so I had a full view of her light blue underwear. I know I turned beet red. She laughed, flipping her skirt back down. "Now you have to show me your wiener."

"What?" I squeaked.

"Your wiener. You know, your business."

I just shook my head.

"Oh, you're no fun. I showed you my panties. You're supposed to show me your thing."

Alice jumped to her feet and hollered, "Stupid!" at the top of her lungs. Then she ran to the school house chanting, "Bobby is a sissy."

Girls weren't quite like cows, I decided.

39: SCHOOLHOUSE DISCIPLINE

Discipline must have been a challenge for a young teacher with sixteen to twenty-two pupils spread across eight grades. Students varied greatly in size as well as developmental issues. Often the oldest student would be a boy who had been held back one or two years, so he could easily be a hulking fifteen-year old. Sitting in a schoolhouse with six-year olds was the last place that young man wanted to be.

Playground supervision often required the teacher to be outside in all kinds of weather to see that everyone was included and that no one was too abused. Obviously, she couldn't be everywhere at once, so there were plenty of opportunities for trouble to arise. And sometimes there were direct challenges to her authority.

Of course not all trouble started on the playground. Spitball fights, refusal to comply with orders, rowdiness, and bad language were some of the ways in which trouble could manifest in the schoolhouse. Mrs. Staples had several options for discipline at her command. She could keep a student after school for fifteen minutes or longer — but that would attract the attention of a parent and was not something she necessarily wanted to do. There were times when she expected peers to enforce the rules on each other by shushing others or talking them back into compliance. Mrs. Staples would also use additional school chores as punishment. A recalcitrant student might have to stay after school and clap the chalkboard erasers until they came clean to her satisfaction. She might try to kid or cajole a student into doing what she wanted him to do.

For bad language, washing out the student's mouth with soap was common practice. I only had this done to me once.

I learned quickly not to say everything I was thinking.

Keeping students in from recess (morning, noon hour, or afternoon) was a ready punishment. Of course, the built-in problem with this punishment was that the teacher had to stay inside and supervise. I missed a lot of noon hours in my first few years of school because I hated peanut butter and jelly sandwiches and I couldn't go out to play until I had finished my lunch. Later on, my mother started using sandwich spreads which were much more tasty. I also had learned the art of trading things I didn't like to eat with others during the morning recess or before school.

At least most of the boys in that one-room schoolhouse carried pocketknives, either in a pocket or in a boot. Those knives were sometimes used for games played in the dirt, or sometimes for whittling. Usually they just stayed in the pockets. I don't remember being threatened, or know of anyone else who was threatened with a knife during those eight years. My first pocketknife was given to me at our school Christmas program by the older girl who had drawn my name.

I don't remember a teacher hitting a student, but there was a day when Mrs. Staples must have come close to losing it. She had been taking abusive language and the "I won't do it" attitude from one of the older boys for several days in a row. She had stuck by this boy when others in the community thought he should be expelled and wasn't worth the effort. He wasn't going to amount to anything anyway — "Just look at his brother," they said.

The boy refused one too many times. Mrs. Staples marched to where he was sitting, pulled him from his desk and declared, "If you're going to treat me like trash, then that's where you're going." She hustled him toward her desk and lifted him upside down into the large trashcan by the desk.

He came out of that can sputtering and staring wildly at Mrs. Staples, who had crossed her arms over her chest like some kind of Amazon. I never knew what he saw when he looked at her, but he started to laugh. Not at her, perhaps at himself, most likely at the situation.

Shortly, she joined him by laughing, also. He allowed himself to be escorted back to his seat where she bowed to him while still smiling. A collective release of breath could be heard from the rest of us before we joined the laughter. The teacher had restored order to the schoolroom.

By the way, this particular young man, after a series of ups and downs, has become a very successful small businessman. I wonder if he still remembers the bottom of the wastebasket. I hope he remembers Mrs. Staples who never gave up on him.

40: BOYS AND GIRLS

I was married at the age of seven. The wedding took place on a Friday night in the shadows of Ben's store. The store was a frequent gathering spot for locals on Friday night. While parents talked with neighbors about crops, weather and upcoming church socials, the children played outside.

My bride was eight, and her sister, older by two years, performed the wedding. There were another half dozen or so kids present. After the wedding we all set to work to construct a house out of cardboard and scrap boards left over from receiving shipments of farm implements and parts. I don't know what was supposed to happen after the house was built. I had to leave before that feat was accomplished. The worst part of the wedding was the kiss.

My parents weren't at all pleased when on the way home I told them about the wedding and about the kiss — I was also divorced at the age of seven.

While the wedding reinforced traditional male-female roles, much of life in the farm community actually blurred those roles. Because there were few of us attending the one room schoolhouse, most games were played without regard to gender or even, for the most part, age: softball, dodge ball, pond pond pullaway, touch football, ante ante over, tag and so on. Particularly younger boys played games usually restricted to girls such as hopscotch, skipping rope, and playing house. Older boys removed themselves from these activities and sometimes snickered, perhaps enviously, at their younger gender mates.

When families visited socially, kids usually played with whatever and whoever was available. If girls came to my house, we played cowboys and Indians, ran trucks and cars up and down the slanted cellar door, swung on the tire swing, climbed trees, or tended a store which I had created with boxes and cans behind the house. If we visited a family with girls, I played with dolls and doll houses, cooked meals on a toy stove, and listened for heartbeats with a doctor's stethoscope. And wherever we were, there was plenty of time for talking about things that mattered and for dreaming about the future. Perhaps, because there were few kids of the same age of any gender, there was less emphasis on playing only with boy things or only with girl things than there might have been in more populous areas.

Cows didn't seem to notice or care whether the person feeding or milking them was male or female. Girls were as capable of driving tractors, cultivating corn, raking hay as were boys. Certainly, there was some heavy work that was beyond most girls, but they often participated quite fully in carrying out the work of the farm. In farm families where there were only girls, few jobs were spared from them because of "feminine sensitivities" including cleaning barn gutters and helping with birthing.

Girls showed beef and dairy, sheep and hogs at county and state fairs alongside boys. Not only did their charges win their share of blue ribbons — frequently, the girls won showmanship awards. Some boys didn't take too kindly to girls beating them in showmanship, but that was the way it was.

As technological labor-saving devices advanced, there was less need for manual labor on the farm, and the girls were the first to be relieved of their barn and outdoor chores, so they could fulfill their responsibilities and roles in the house. Looking back, I expect the decrease of girls and young women working in the barns and fields was a blow to equality on the farm and within the farm community. It probably also smothered the impact of the imagination and dreams which many young females brought to the farming enterprise.

41: OLD WOMAN FISHING

The bobber rides the ripples —
    rising, lowering.

Several feet below the water's surface,
    a worm wiggles to free itself
    from death's grasp.

The old woman holding the cane pole
    waits patiently,
        one finger wrapped around the line,
            poised.

The old woman daydreams alertly
    of other lakes and rivers
    of worms enticing food
        when cupboards were bare
    of children learning to wield
        a cane pole
            three and four times their size
    of grandchildren doing
        the same.

Laughter echoes across the
    waters of time.

Tears: past, present and future
    merge at the water's edge.

42 WORRY

I don't know about you, but I have probably spent far too much energy on worrying during my lifetime. When I was young my dad called me a worry-wart. I never knew if that meant persons who worry would get a lot of warts, or whether persons who worry are somehow related to warthogs. But I did worry a fair amount.

I worried about my size, about making friends in new settings, about how awkward I must look attempting to dance, about moustache hair or the lack thereof, and about girls (I worried a lot about girls). I worried about what I would be when I grew up and why it was taking so long to get there.

Over the years I've worried a lot about my children and their worries, about my parents and their worries, and now there are grandchildren. I try not to worry about them, but with little success.

43: RAKING HAY

One of my first jobs on the farm after learning how to drive a tractor was raking hay. This was a fairly simple task involving driving the tractor straight along a swath of freshly cut hay. The rake would follow wherever the tractor led. With its long narrow teeth spinning round and round, the rake would pick up the flat hay and pitch it into neat long rows — sort of like large long ropes of hay. It now being fluffed up into windrows, the hay would hopefully dry and be baled before the next rain.

The source of a straight windrow of hay was to be found in the person guiding the tractor. Sometimes, however, tractors and rakes seemed to have minds of their own. The front tires might hit a half hidden rock throwing the tractor and therefore the rake off course, or the driver might spy a hawk and glance away for a moment too long. Crooked windrows were the result, and meant that valuable hay was left flat upon the ground to spoil and waste.

The judge of "raking competency" was my father, who had a very keen eye for waste.

44: PUBLIC SPEAKING

My initial attempts at public speaking were anything but auspicious.

I was three when I stood before a small Christmas Eve crowd to recite my first piece, "What A Good Boy Am I." Terrified is a weak word to describe my churning innards. Somehow I squeaked the words out. Many of those big people sitting in front of me cupped their ears as if they were hard of hearing.

While still swallowing the last syllable, I dashed for my mother who sat four rows from the front. My actions were greeted with laughter and a smattering of applause. I knelt before my mother, laid my head upon her lap and sobbed as quietly as I could manage. She shushed me and patted my back, but I was beyond consoling. I had failed. Would Santa leave only coal in my sock?

My first experiences in grade school were not much better. When practicing my little "pieces" for the school Christmas program — one of the high points of the school year and for the entire community — I would stutter. I seldom stammered at other times. Some of the kids poked fun at me. My brother stood up for me during those first two years before he graduated from the one-room schoolhouse. I learned years later that he had had an even more severe experience with stuttering when he started school.

It was Mrs. Staples who helped me chase the feared demons away. Rather than having me recite "pieces," she had me take roles in the plays that we put on during the program. Usually, these were short comedies. I quickly caught on that if I pretended well enough to be a particular character and if I resisted peeking at the audience crowding the small schoolhouse, I could not only get by, I actually enjoyed this kind of "public speaking." The crowd wasn't laughing at me, but rather at the antics of my character, and their laughter meant that I was performing well.

45: SHEPHERDS QUAKE

Christmas programs at the church were less worldly than those at the school. Programs at the school, though, often ended with the "nativity scene." These were days, at least in rural areas, where no one questioned the propriety of having an explicit Christian message conclude a public school program.

The nativity scene, however, was not only the end of the Sunday School program — it was what the entire program built up to. It was to be the solemn pinnacle, reminding everyone of what Christmas was really about.

Some of us who had appropriate pieces or recitations that we had learned for the school program were asked to deliver them again, even though most everyone at church had heard them earlier in the week over at the schoolhouse. Unlike the school nativity scene, the Sunday School scene was narrated. Usually an older boy was given this job; sometimes it was shared with an older girl, and when those arms weren't successfully twisted, an adult filled in.

Everyone, from the youngest child to the oldest youth, had a role. There was always room for one more angel for the girls or one more shepherd for the boys. The number of wise men never varied, but fortunately no one claimed to know how many angels or shepherds appeared that night in Bethlehem.

The role girls sought most was that of Mary. The role most boys dreaded was that of Joseph. Girls often went out of their way to be Mary and then begged the adults in charge to choose a certain boy for Joseph. With the sanctuary darkened but for intensely bright flashlights shining on the manger and on the star, Mary would beam radiantly, pleased with being at the center of attention next to the boy she most wanted to notice her, while Joseph's eyes flitted about as if trying to locate his donkey.

A heavy curtain separated parents, relatives and friends from the stage. Behind the curtain was much shushing by teachers and older girls who were practicing to be teachers. Out front, neighbors chattered with neighbors without interventions to keep them quiet. The wire holding the curtain up broke two years in a row. After that the curtain wasn't used again and the adults in the audience felt more compelled to remain quiet as the stage was set.

One year stands out in my memory. Everything looked fine, even after the angels and shepherds arrived on the scene. Of course, Mary and Joseph had come first to kneel behind a crude manger. On real straw lay a plastic doll. Sometimes it wasn't particularly obvious that the doll was supposed to be a girl or a boy. Many of the older kids would try to check that out. Usually a Sunday School teacher would express horror while re-wrapping the babe.

Anyway, as the wise men arrived with their gifts and claimed space for themselves on the stairs much of the tableau shifted a step or two backwards to make room. It was always much more difficult to see in the near darkness and shadows than during practice when the lights glared. We never found out whether it was a shepherd's crook or the halo of one of the older girls, but something knocked against the lowest point of the star, which hung on a long wire from a nail high up on the back wall. Unbeknownst to us in the nativity scene, the star began to swing back and forth like a pendulum. In the Sunday School room off the sanctuary, a boy straddled a ladder holding a huge flashlight, shining it at the star. Each time the Bethlehem Star swayed one direction he did the same, determined to do what he had been instructed: "Keep that flashlight on the star — don't shine it on the wall."

The tittering from some in the crowd didn't fit the response we expected to this solemn scene.

We, naturally, had been taught not to make a sound or to move until the crowd concluded singing *Silent Night*. We heard a loud crash from the Sunday School room and the light of the Bethlehem Star went out. No angel, shepherd, or wise man flinched. Mary's smiled stayed in place. I was told later that Joseph's face had that "I didn't do it" look on it.

Without waiting for the narrator to finish his script, the pageant director leapt to the stage where the piano stood and immediately began playing *Silent Night*. By the end of the second verse, we were being motioned to begin our march down the middle of the sanctuary. It felt more like a retreat.

We received lots of praise from parents and teachers. Some couldn't quite stop laughing. We knew that before the next Christmas program some changes would be made to the star and the manner by which it was lit.

There were suspicions voiced that the fluttering of the Bethlehem Star hadn't occurred entirely by accident. Had it really been caused by a shepherd's crook or by an askew angel's halo? Accident or intentional?

I wouldn't tell, if I knew.

46: CRAYONS ON A DESK

Crayons. Bought before the 4th of July, if I could. My folks always said, "you can't buy school supplies until after the 4th of July or there won't be any left for school."

Those crayons were so exotic. Not just reds, blacks, whites — but pinks, grays, oranges and something called chartreuse. They seemed fat. Hard to hold on to. Were they clumsy, or was I? They smelled sharp and distinctive. Tasted pasty, if I remember right.

Sally and I would color pages of coloring books the teacher brought to school. We colored stick figures on wide lined tablets. Sally taught me how to use a dictionary and the encyclopedia. She was very bright. Although she was ahead of me in school, we still competed with each other: at spelling, arithmetic, hopscotch, softball, running and spitting. At times we would fight and at other times she would take me under her wing sort of protecting me like an older sister.

We were together in grade school until Sally's folks died. Their car hit a patch of ice and slammed into a tree. That was the winter of the long hard freeze. Palmyra Lake lost most of its fish that year. Mr. Brown, down the road, had two cows freeze in place. Just stood there till they died.

I heard of Sally later when I was a senior in high school. They said she would do most anything you wanted for $5.00. Kinda like Mr. Brown's cows, I guess. She froze up too — that winter of the long, hard freeze.

47: NEAR MISSES

    Safety — whether it be not walking across the grass barefoot (there could be nails and sharp glass or lumber anywhere), how best to ride on a wagon or tractor, not walking too close behind the cows or horses, how to handle a shotgun, wearing gloves, not having loose clothing on around machinery, looking away from the welding machine when the blacksmith sharpened a mower sickle or a plow shear, not accepting rides from strangers, not coasting too fast down the hill toward Punk, being prepared to lay flat in a ditch in the face of a tornado — was drummed into me by both my parents from the time I could understand.
    There was good reason for concern. Living on a farm means living in a potentially dangerous place. Our family had its share of near misses and we knew of other families in our community who were not as fortunate.
    Danger often happens suddenly. There was the afternoon Dad was unharnessing Dolly and Molly from the corn planter in front of the machine shed. The rain was already coming down hard. Then the wind blew the shed door off. The panicked horses reared and pawed, and could easily have run my dad over.
    Each of us, including my mother, had the experience of getting fingers nearly caught in a drive belt or of getting too close to a whirling blower that blew the silage up a long pipe to the silo. Occasionally, the blower would be plugged with too much silage and instead of walking to the tractor to shut off the fan belt driving the blower, we'd use a bent fork to pull the excess silage a way. Usually, that worked. Sometimes, the fork would get too close to the whirling blower and be pulled out of our hands. Too often the hands followed the

fork too closely. Or sometimes, we stupidly tried to clean out the excess with our hands instead of using a fork.

Lightning strikes were a common problem; not only was the accompanying crack and thunder ear-splitting, life and property were at risk. Several times after a storm, we'd go out to check on the herd and find a cow lying prone with all four legs rigid — not a good sign at all. The rendering truck was one of the least favorite sights on the farm, but dead animals had to be removed. Cows and horses were too large to bury. Both house and barn were protected with lightning rods. On numerous occasions, we'd find carbon on aluminum milk strainers and utensils in the milkhouse. The electric current had followed a water pipe.

There was a small section of the farm bordering the marsh that contained quicksand. We never pastured our cows in that field, but once in a while cows would wear down a barbed wire fence or realize that an electric fence had been grounded out by a weed, and then decide that indeed the grass was greener on the other side of the fence. On one such occasion, we had a cow step into quicksand. By the time help arrived only her neck, head and topline were visible and she was bellowing fiercely. With ropes, a tractor, and help from neighbors, the cow was eventually rescued.

And then there was the day Ma nearly burned the house down. One afternoon, she burned some garbage at the edge of the orchard, which she did every so often to keep the garbage pile under control. I was in school and my dad and brother were at the feed mill. As my mother was beginning to prepare supper, she glanced out a kitchen window and saw smoke. She ran outside and saw that much of the orchard was on fire and the yard bordering the west side of the house was burning. My dad and my brother roared into the driveway at about the same time. They had seen the smoke from a half mile away. Together with shovels, wet burlap bags, and rakes they put out the fire and saved the house. The volunteer fire department, four miles away, would never have arrived in time.

Cows could kick you or step on you. Some seemed to enjoy doing it. One such cow was named "Kicker." My mother had more than one rooster peck her fingers or hen claw at her to protect its eggs. A ram sheep tried to use my dad who was bent over attending to something on the ground as a battering ram — that was the last day we had a male sheep. And we never owned a bull. Dad had had one in Illinois, but it was just too dangerous to have a bull on the property. Thus my dad was one of the pioneers in southeastern Wisconsin in establishing a breeders' co-op that offered artificial insemination services.

The potential for accidents, for danger, permeated the farm, yet we didn't live in fear. We were taught to be cautious in order to prevent the likelihood of an accident. And when the unexpected happened, we tried to respond quickly and calmly.

48: PREACHING TO THE COWS

Imagination had free rein on the farm. Damsels in distress and knights in shining armor appeared along with a panoply of other storybook characters in the white clouds moving gradually across a robin's egg blue sky. Pebbles made adequate baseballs and a rough two by two served well as a bat. Tobacco weed seeds looked exactly like ground coffee. Animal pathways through the woods were old Indian trails. Dashing up the steep grassy back slope of the gravel pit mirrored Pickett's Charge at Gettysburg.

Once school was out for the summer, I seldom saw other kids. I was left with my growing list of chores, but there was always time for reading books and of course for imagining what had been and what might be. My dad and brother sometimes complained that I daydreamed too much, but I learned early on that in one's own mind places could be created and stories could be told that were not subject to the whims of others.

If books were the lifeblood of my youth, which I believe they were, then imagination was the breath or life force. I read everything I could get hold of from The Bobbsey Twins series to *Little Women,* from Zane Grey novels to Mitchner's *Hawaii,* from Trixie Belden mysteries to Tom Swift and Tom Swift, Jr. science fiction. And of course I read the Bible.

The school was a natural cauldron for bringing my imagination to a boil. More books and more books were read. My teacher brought in books from her book club, once I had exhausted the supply in the schoolhouse. She encouraged us to dream of far away places like Switzerland and the Matterhorn, to imagine ourselves as doctors, lawyers, forest rangers, veterinarians, teachers, farmers, and anything else we might think of, and to roam the possibilities of the unknown. We were never told that any dream was out of reach because we were rural, too backward, or too poor. Imaginations were set free as we reenacted great events such as Lincoln's Gettysburg Address or when we drew "our feelings" or experiences while listening to symphonies played on radio educational programs.

The schoolyard was also rich with fantasy. Cowboys and Indians was played by boys and girls alike. In the fall, forts were built from saplings and brush. In the winter, large blocks of snow were shaped just right to form snow forts. Usually, we were allowed to carry water from the pump to help the blocks freeze in place. These forts had to be built close enough so snowballs could carry from one fort to the other. Once the forts were prepared, we could reenact famous battles that we'd heard of such as the World War II Battle of the Bulge or the Korean War Battle of Porkchop Hill. These rather aggressive fantasies were balanced with making angels in the snow, pretending that hopscotch was a dance dating back to the Colonial period of Johnny Tremain, and swooping across the yard with arms extended like giant eagles in order to see the world through their eyes.

It was preaching to the cows, however, that has the strongest grip on my recollection of childhood imaginings. I was perhaps eight or nine years old when I would walk to a long sloping grassy side of the gravel pit where our cows often grazed. There I would stand near the top of the slope and preach to the cows. In my mind's eye I was standing on a hill overlooking the Sea of Galilee preaching about Jesus and his love. And the cows were eager enough listeners. At least they never complained. Occasionally, a couple cows would fall asleep. And once in a while one got up and walked away.

Decades later, I was on sabbatical at St. George's College in Jerusalem. During the course of my stay, our group of pilgrims had two worship services, one at Bethlehem and the other on the shores of the Sea of Galilee. At our first meeting, the director of the program announced that he had assigned various tasks to individuals and we could check on the bulletin board to see what he would like us to do. If we wanted to decline we could do so.

Before even seeing my assignment, I made up my mind to decline. I'm not particularly comfortable in strange groups; my preferred position is in the back, so I can better observe what is happening. And, I was on sabbatical. I didn't want to do a prayer, read scriptures, or anything else. I just wanted to soak up the atmosphere of Israel and imagine how it must have been during the time of Jesus.

After lunch, when no one else was around, I walked up to the bulletin board to see if I had been assigned anything to do. My jaw dropped when I saw my name penciled in by "Sea of Galilee — Sermon." I pulled my pencil out immediately and pressed the eraser against my name. Then the image of an eight year old boy preaching to the cows flashed before my eyes. Groaning, I stuffed the pencil back in my pocket.

Preaching to a group of some forty folks by the Sea of Galilee turned out to be one of the most humbling and gratifying experiences that I have ever had. It was beyond my adult imagination. Yet as a child, free to imagine at will, I had done just that.

49: THE SILO

A forty-foot tall concrete cylinder, higher than the barn it stood. Next to it was a twin. When it was empty, a man could stand in its pit and still climb out; I couldn't.

Nothing smelled better on the farm than fresh corn silage. Perhaps it was the silage fermenting that yielded such pungent, embracing odors. On a star-lit, frosty morning I would open the barn door to be greeted by the welcoming fragrance.

Small boards just the right size would be fitted together inside the iron handholds that made a ladder, tongues in grooves, rising toward the roof foot by foot, as the silo was newly filled. It was not difficult climbing to the top rung by rung on the inside, for it was like going upward in a rather small concrete tube. There was no danger of falling over backwards. But it was still a long way down to the concrete floor if feet slipped from the iron rungs.

Climbing the outside ladder up the silo to fit the blower pipe into the silo window was an entirely different matter. This required rope, strength from those pulling on the rope to hoist the pipe up the silo wall, and a lot of nerve on the part of the climber. My dad performed the high silo work for years and then my brother did it. I never did. I still get a little queasy with heights.

In January the silage was frozen thick. A pickaxe was needed to chop chunks small enough to drop down the shaft. Wheelbarrow loads would then be hauled to the center of the barn where the ice would melt, leaving valuable feed for the cows. This was hard work. As I got older, I would swing the pick. It would often take several swings before a crack would appear in the solid frozen tundra of silage.

By late spring, the silo would be nearly empty and the odors issuing forth from the concrete fortress were beyond bold and wild. These would assault the nostrils which tried to squeeze shut long enough to pitch the now very juicy silage up and over the doorway. Fermentation had taken its toll on the corn; at this point it could have rivaled the potency of the worst white lightning from the Tennessee hill country.

The silo was a very private, secure place as there was only one entrance and no one could possibly sneak up to whatever level the silage might be. This was the place where an out-of season pheasant was temporarily stored. Here cigarette and pipe smoke would not be detected. Here the wildest fantasies could be played out without prying eyes.

Yes, those circular walls of concrete were strange, foreboding, and enticing.

50: LEFTOVERS!

"Leftovers! Again?" These were thoughts expressed daily in the mind, but never verbalized as I grew up. The noontime meal was the big meal on the farm. Supper was usually a mixture of something new with leftovers from the noon meal. Too often it was simply leftovers. Delicious boiled potatoes at noon became fried potatoes at supper. Crisp beans at noon became wilted, tasteless bean look-alikes for supper. The mouth watering beef roast at noon became cold, crusty beef with white lard-like stuff to be cut away for supper. Such were my impressions of leftovers. Leftovers were bad news indeed!

Try as hard as my brother and I could, we could never eat enough at noon to be certain that there would be no leftovers for supper. I sometimes thought Ma had learned Jesus' secret with those seven loaves and two fishes. She never failed to perform the miracle in the farmhouse — the much awaited noon meal would somehow reappear as dreaded leftovers for supper.

Now, I must admit that I have not spent a lifetime worrying about leftovers. I have done a reasonable job of integrating these childhood leftovers anxieties into an adult life which is okay with a leftover, now and then. Still, I find it better to finish a meal and start anew with the next. It may be too much to expect a good thing to last forever — that is, until the next meal.

51: CHRISTMAS EVE

Anticipation filled the air during the entire Christmas season; it was at its peak on Christmas Eve Day.

Dreaming about Christmas began with the arrival of the Sears Christmas catalog, usually sometime in October. It was a smaller sized catalog than the standard, but it was read, looked at, and admired much, much more. The toy section alone must have covered twenty pages — cowboy outfits and holsters and cap guns, train sets (electric and windup), trucks and caterpillars, toy soldiers and fighter planes, games and balsam models, baseball gloves and footballs, erector sets and tinker toys. That little catalog had everything a young boy might dream of having.

Of course, the catalog was also used to choose gifts for others in the family. Ma and I would sit at the kitchen table and make those selections: a handkerchief for Grandma; gloves for Dad; socks for my brother. Dad would help me later find some perfume or a handkerchief for Ma.

But no question about it, the Sears catalog served primarily to fan dreams of what Santa might bring on Christmas morning. As the season approached, it was necessary to whittle down the wish list so a letter could be sent to Santa. I always printed that letter even after I could do script writing because I didn't want to take the chance that Santa might not be able to read my handwriting. Penmanship was always my lowest grade in school.

By Christmas Eve, the tree had been decorated for a couple weeks and packages ringed its base. When I was really young many of the decorations were cardboard. Some years we'd string popcorn and hang them on the tree. I only remember seeing real candles lit on the tree once. After that there were strings of lights — often tangled, sometimes not working, but clearly safer. A star or an angel usually sat at the very top of the tree. I always wanted to be tall enough to stand on a chair in order to attach that ornament, but I had to wait to grow a lot and for my brother to leave home.

It was always wise to check the colorful packages under the tree daily because new ones appeared without any announcement. Our family exchanged its presents to one another on Christmas Eve and Christmas morning was left to Santa.

Ma was at least as excited about Christmas as anyone in the family. Every year she would try to get my dad to agree for each of us to open a package early on Christmas Eve day. She would enlist my support as well as my brother's. We would plead and beg and she'd smile and say, "What a great idea!" Dad would usually grouse about it and not give in, though there were occasional exceptions when each of us opened a present at three in the afternoon. Ma could not have been happier, and I was pretty pleased myself. But usually we had to wait.

There was one Christmas Eve before I was old enough to work in the barn that Ma's and my curiosity almost got the best of us. My dad and brother were out milking the cows. There was no more fudge to make, no more cookies to bake.

After staring at those packages and trying to guess what was in them, Ma and I had to shake them one more time. I hefted one present about the size of a shoebox. That one was to me from my brother. I shook the box and it rattled. I shook it again and a blue and yellow metal truck dropped out onto my lap.

My jaw dropped and I hollered, "Oh no!"

Ma's hand flew to her mouth but could not hide her laughter.

Scowling, Grandma scolded, "Told you, you shouldn't be playing with those presents. What would your dad do if he could see you?"

"It's okay!" exclaimed Ma. "I'll hurry and rewrap it. Just don't tell your dad and brother." She glanced at Grandma.

Grandma folded her arms and grunted.

I tried to look really surprised an hour later when I opened the package containing that blue and yellow truck. It must have worked. Nobody said a word about the mishap, not even Grandma.

52: THE FUNERAL

The window shades on the north side of the school were drawn; those on the south side remained up, allowing afternoon sunshine to spill into the room. Light and shadows merged and parted in unusual ways.

Sixth graders were reading their lessons at the front of the room in hushed tones. I and two other third graders practiced our penmanship without whispering. Even the promptings from Mrs. Staples were quieter than normal.

Maintaining concentration on a book, printing one's name, or working a cross-word puzzle with a friend was difficult. The movement of the clock's hands vibrated across the room. The smell of chalk dusk and hectograph ink was intense. Everyone was going to the bubbler often, perhaps because of dry throats. No one raised a hand to ask to go to the outhouse. Everyone knew such a request would be denied. We had all been sent there half an hour earlier, whether we had to go or not.

No one questioned why the window shades were pulled. We all knew that just across our playground fence, Mr. Bonner was being laid in the ground. Some wanted to peek under a shade, but no one dared. Most of us had never been to a funeral. We could only imagine what was happening next to where we had eaten our lunch.

Earlier in the morning, during recess, we had seen two men digging the hole for the grave. They worked very hard. To our surprise, when their work was done they sat down right next to the grave to smoke their cigarettes. They didn't look very scary really. But neither did they smile at us when we waved. Mrs. Staples called us away from the fence to the other side of the schoolhouse.

I knew old Mr. Bonner, as did many of the kids. He lived down the hill. I pedaled by his little, rickety house to and from school. A lot of folks thought he was a bit strange. We weren't allowed to go there at Halloween. He didn't go to our church. I never saw any kids in his yard, though it was hard to see through the overgrown bushes. Once in a while I would see him at Ben's store. He never said anything to me. He always grinned, though it looked like his grin was about to fall off the side of his face. Some of the older kids would make faces at him; I never did that.

There was sadness in the schoolhouse. Nobody talked of Mr. Bonner or of what was happening outside. Still, little Annie had been crying. You could tell because her eyes and cheeks looked red like she had just come in from a frosty wintry day, but it was a warm autumn afternoon.

My dad was at the cemetery. I had heard him talking to Ma the night before. "I best go to Bonner's funeral. Don't know if anyone else will, besides the preacher. He had more between his ears than most folks know. Seems like somebody ought to be there to remember."

Well, we in the schoolhouse were remembering, but that didn't count.

Mrs. Staples checked the clock every so often. Finally, she got up, raised a shade, and looked out the window. "All right students, we will take our afternoon recess. It's okay to go to the toilet now."

53: CHURCH SOCIALS

Some might believe that church life revolves around prayer. In my childhood, I knew for certain that church life revolved around food. There were monthly Ladies Aid Society dinners that brought most of the men out of the fields for a couple hours. Often, we at the school house were allowed to go over to the church and carry back a meal for our lunch.

A grand time was had whenever a young man or woman from the community was to be married. Showers, as they were called, were opportunities for the community to gather to give presents to the couple, to offer entertainment, and, of course, to share food. These were the evenings when a soloist might sing love songs and then lead everyone in such standbys as *She'll Be Comin' Round the Mountain, You Are My Sunshine, O' Susannah, I Dream of Jeannie*. Older couples smiled and laughed at each other reliving their own memories, and no one seemed to care if some weren't so good at carrying a tune.

Box Socials were not my favorites because I was never certain with whom I would end up eating. The fancy wrapped boxes filled with food sat on a table at the front of the church dining room. Dad was usually an auctioneer or spotter so he and his best friend generally made certain that I got the box prepared by my best friend. There were occasions when someone — I always suspected my brother and his friends — replaced the identifying bow so I had to sit with someone much older. Most people seemed to have a good time at these functions. In particular, the older youth and young adults would bid feverishly, trying to outbid each other while believing that they knew whose box they were bidding on. None of this made much sense to me because most of the time husbands wound up eating with their wives anyway.

Nearly every dinner at the church was pot luck. You could typically depend upon the same person bringing homemade bread, or Jello, or fried chicken, or devil's food cake. It seemed as if each woman had her assigned dish to pass and if any given woman changed her mind and cooked something new, she upset the culinary apple cart.

The exceptions to the potlucks were the Anniversary Dinner in the spring and the Harvest Supper in the fall. For these socials, women baked and cooked for days. Nothing was left to chance. Committees were formed to make sure there would be plenty of food and variety. People from around the surrounding communities would come to these two events. Tickets were sold at the door and lines could often be seen for three to four hours. Although these large undertakings usually went very smoothly from the public's viewpoint, there were the usual glitches and hurt feelings that often took weeks to mend afterwards. One of the things I liked best about these "big dinners" was that my dad was sometimes responsible for the ice cream. How could you have a church social without ice cream? And because you never wanted to run out of ice cream, there often were a few gallon containers left over. Of course, my dad would buy one or two of those gallons and we'd eat ice cream for a month.

Now, I don't want to mislead the reader. There was plenty of prayer in our little church — there were prayers of thanksgiving, prayers for forgiveness, prayers for a bountiful harvest and prayers for health — but, I expect it was more likely food that bound us together.

54: SNAKES ALIVE

I am walking from the barn to the house. I see Ma in the driveway next door talking with our renter, Kathleen. Her two children run up to them excitedly pointing toward the road. As I approach our house, Ma screams. The children scramble to hide behind their mother and then peek from behind her dress, looking back toward the road.

Ma turns and sees me. She shouts, "Run and get your dad's gun. There's a snake at the end of the driveway. Hurry!"

I dash into the house and open the closet door. Tucked in the way back is my dad's twelve gauge Winchester pump. I have shot tin cans with it before. I have walked with my dad while he hunted. Next fall I will be twelve, old enough to carry a gun and really go hunting. I grab the shotgun, reach into the tattered, stained hunting coat, and pull out two shells.

Hurrying back outside, I cross over our driveway and then a small stretch of lawn, into the renters' driveway. The women and children are where they were before as if frozen in cement. Ma points down the length of the driveway. There, stretched across the gravel, is a snake five or six feet long. I had seldom seen a snake, even a garter snake. Poisonous snakes were not supposed to exist in southern Wisconsin.

Ma clearly doesn't care if the snake is poisonous or not. She wants it dead.

I carefully load the two shells into the shotgun even while Ma urges, "hurry, hurry." My dad had taught me much about gun safety. Remembering his advice serves as a counterbalance to Ma's near panic. I hear his words: "Take your time. Only aim at what you want to shoot."

Having loaded the gun, I raise it to my shoulder. Ma, perhaps having second thoughts, says, "Be careful, Bobby."

I sight down the barrel as if I am shooting a tin can. The middle of the snake comes into line with the barrel. I breathe slowly and squeeze the trigger smoothly. My shoulder drops back from the kick of the gun.

The snake is severed in half. I cannot believe my eyes. Ma screams. The neighbor family runs toward their house. The front half of the snake is coming directly at me with its mouth and fangs wide open. Without thinking, I pump the second shell into the chamber, sight and pull the trigger.

The snake's head is never found. His rattles are saved for years to come.

55: PUSSY WILLOW

Behind the barn, beyond the gravel pit hill, across the twenty-acre field where Dad once killed a rattlesnake, down the steep drop-off to the dark fertile soil where potatoes grew, to the edge of the marsh. Through and around overhanging brush — very easy to get turned about in here — avoiding large pools of mud and quicksand. Crossing deer trails and rabbit runs, slipping off bog after bog, moving quietly by the muskrat house and the ducks hunkered down at the pond's edge to the trickle of a small stream — water running swift and clear. Near the top of a remaining snowdrift, a frozen reminder of the winter nearly forgotten, encased in frozen melt, are the buds of a pussy willow.

The pussy willow is a bridge between the darkness of winter and the panoply of color proclaiming spring. It has not the radiant beauty of the tulip; nor does it announce a new season through delightful song as might the robin. Yet the pussy willow, with its subtle softness, with its appearance of fragility contrasted with strength and fortitude, speaks of change, of a new day, of hope.

And thus the pussy willow branches are received with a smile and a warm heart by the woman upon whom the young boy bestows his hard-won treasure.

56: THE BARN REVISITED
(2001)

The barn —
  What a thing of beauty it was
    fifty years ago.

Now it remains a mere skeleton of its former self.
  Once bright red, it is colorless.
  The slanted roof which protected hay and cattle alike
    sags, threatening to implode and suffocate
      any within.
  Twenty-foot long boards randomly absent from the east wall
    make the wind its most permanent resident.
  Toothless, the barn awaits its death.

No one cares enough to refurbish, or even to tear it down.
  For some, the hollow hulk is a reminder of times past:
    of herds, of families, of community tragedies and joys,
      of the way things were.
  To others, it is an ugly eyesore totally out of step
    with the changing landscape.

The barn once stood as the beehive of farm life.
  It is now a precarious gravestone
    hovering over fading memories.

New and Recent Releases from
Singing River Publications

***Reflections Through Black Ice*, by Christine Moroni**
Reflections on the seasons of the year — seasons of the human heart — designed to be read in the early morning light of sunrise or by the glow of evening twilight.

***Cow Pies & Bases*, by Robert B. Coates**
Warm, funny, poignant and engaging, this book offers an honest, unabashed account of growing up in rural mid-America just after World War II.

***Let Your Light Shine*, by Ann King Lishinski**
A richly illustrated book for children of all ages to remind us that anything is possible if we try, and that we live on in ways we never could have foreseen.

***Jordan's Near Side*, by Frank Stafford Davis**
Windows into how the Sacred manifests in nature and in the ordinariness of our daily lives, drawn from the author's experience as a parish pastor on Minnesota's Mesabi Iron Range.

Available through:
   Singing River Publications
   P.O. Box 72
   Ely, MN 55731
   www.speravi.com/singingriver